Table of Contents

DEDICATION

This book is dedicated to the members of our church, The Abundant Living Faith Center. I love you and thank God for you. The confidence and trust you have expressed in Rochelle and me inspires us to do more in the Kingdom of God.

WISDOM
&
GUIDANCE

Charles Nieman

WORD OF FAITH
LEADERSHIP AND BIBLE INSTITUTE

All Scripture quotations
from the King James Version
of the Bible unless otherwise stated

ISBN 0-914307-19-3

Printed in the United States of America
Copyright © 1983 WORD OF FAITH PUBLISHING
PO Box 819000, Dallas, Texas 75381

INTRODUCTION

Wisdom and guidance. When you think of one, you generally think of the other. The two terms go together in our thinking and rightfully so. Many times when we speak of needing guidance in a particular situation, we express it by saying, "I need God's wisdom in order to know what to do." Solomon said that the wisdom of God is the most important thing that a child of God can obtain in life. He also said that God's wisdom is crying out in the streets and and in the chief places of concourse. In other words, His wisdom is available for everyone. Each of us can have God's wisdom for life in our life.

For years the area of guidance has been covered over with a cloak of mystery in the church. I can not think of another area that has been so "spiritualized" by Christians. Several of Christianity's favorite doctrines revolve around guidance. In this book I have endeavored to remove that cloak of mystery and show the believer how he or she can know God's will *for* and *in* their life.

Chapter I

WALKING IN THE WISDOM OF GOD

Ephesians 5:1, *"Be ye therefore followers of God as dear children: And walk in love, as Christ hath loved us, and hath given himself for us an offering and a sacrifice to God for a sweetsmelling savour. But fornication, and all uncleanness, or covetousness, let it not be once named among you, as becometh saints."* Whether you realize it or not, you are already a saint. *"Neither filthiness, nor foolish talking, nor jesting, which are not convenient: but rather giving of thanks. For this ye know, that no whoremonger, nor unclean person, nor covetous man, who is an idolater. . . ."* Notice God considers being covetous the same as being an idolater. There are a lot of people who would never worship idols, but they are still covetous. God calls it the same thing. You must be careful with covetousness. It can slip upon you easily.

1

"For this ye know, that no whoremonger, nor unclean person, nor covetous man, who is an idolater, hath any inheritance in the kingdom of Christ and of God. Let no man deceive you with vain words: for because of these things cometh the wrath of God . . . " We hear a lot today on the radio and television about the wrath of God coming upon this nation. I hear it constantly. But I want you to see upon whom the wrath of God comes. It comes upon the children of disobedience. It does not come upon those who are obedient to God's Word. Stop laying in bed at night worrying about the wrath of God coming upon you. If you are disobedient, then become obedient. It is just that simple. If you are disobedient, lying in bed worrying won't change things. You need to correct yourself and become obedient.

"Be not ye therefore partakers with them. For ye were sometimes darkness, but now are ye light in the Lord: walk as children of light." He did not say that you sometimes walked in darkness, although the second chapter of Ephesians does say that. He said that at one time in your life you were darkness. You were darkness itself. It was not just that you were in the dark — you were darkness. It was your nature. But now, praise God, you are light! You are not merely in the light, you are light. *"For ye were sometimes darkness, but — now are ye light in the Lord: walk as children of light."*

Before we read any further in this chapter I want to cross reference some scriptures in John 8. John 8:12, *"Then spake Jesus again unto them, saying, I am the light of the world . . . "* We would all agree that He is the light of the world. *". . . he that followeth me* (Are you following him? Then he is talking about you.) *shall not*

2

walk in darkness. . . " If you stopped right there you would think that His next statement would be "but, he shall walk in the light." That is not what He says, *". . . he that followeth me shall not walk in darkness, but shall have the light of life."* We actually have the light in us. What a difference that makes! If you have the light in you, then you will not depend upon light from an outside source. You can go anywhere, in any kind of darkness, and have the light within you.

Jesus, speaking in Matthew 5:13, said, *"Ye are the salt of the earth: but if the salt has lost his savour, wherewith shall it be salted? it is thenceforth good for nothing, but to be cast out, and to be trodden under foot of men. Ye are the light of the world. . . "* In John 8 He said He was the light of the world, but in Matthew 5 He says you are the light of the world.

How can you be the light of the world and He be the light of the world? Because you and He are one. What he is, you now are in this world. Look what else He says about you. Verse 14, *"Ye are the light of the world. A city that is set on an hill cannot be hid."* You cannot hide a city set on the side of a hill. Now watch what He said in respect to that. *"Neither do men light a candle, and put it under a bushel. . . "* In other words, God did not send you into the earth as light of the world and then hide you or cover you up. You are not supposed to hide your light. You are supposed to take your light out into the world. It should not just stay in the church house. *". . . but on a candlestick; and it giveth light unto all that are in the house. Let your light so shine before men. . . "* Why? Why does God want your light to shine? *". . . that they may see your good works. . . "* Wait a minute — good works and light shining have something to do with each other — don't they? *". . . and glorify your Father which is in heaven."* When does God receive glory? When men see your good works. If men see your good works, what are you doing? You are letting your light shine. Your light is the light of the world — so men are drawn to God when your good works shine. Do not ever apologize for testifying to the good works of God in your life. You are letting your light shine.

Let's read again in Ephesians 5 verse 8. *"For ye were sometimes darkness, but now are ye light in the Lord: walk as children of light: For the fruit of the Spirit is in all goodness and righteousness and truth."* He said for us to walk as children of the light, *"Proving what is acceptable unto the Lord."* We are supposed to prove what is acceptable unto the Lord. *"And have no fellowship* (What is fellowship? It is common interests and common desires.) *with the unfruitful works of darkness. . . "* Verse 9, *"For the fruit of the Spirit is in all goodness and righteousness and truth."* The fruit we are to bear is goodness, righteousness, and truth. *"And have no fellowship with the unfruitful works of darkness, but rather reprove them. For it is a shame even to speak of those things which are done of them in secret. But all things that are reproved are made manifest by the light. . . "* Who is the light? The church is the light. The light manifests the unfruitful works of darkness. Then, through being manifested, they are reproved. That is a part of what the church does in the earth. As our light shines it is going to manifest the fruits of darkness, and when they are manifested they will be reproved. The church is persecuted because men love darkness and do not

4

want their deeds manifested. It makes them uncomfortable. "*. . . for whatsoever doth make manifest is light. Wherefore he saith, Awake thou that sleepest. . .* Someone who is sleeping is in the dark. You may be in a light room; but inside of you it is dark when you are asleep.

"*. . . Awake thou that sleepest, and arise from the dead,* (Someone who is dead is really in the dark!) *and Christ shall give thee light.*" Here the Bible shows us an interesting truth. You can be alive and dead at the same time. All of us were dead when we were still living. We were dead in our trespasses and sins. Ephesians chapter 2 tells us that. We were walking around breathing, talking, joking, and having a big time, but spiritually we were dead. Then we were awakened by the light of the glorious Gospel. II Corinthians 4 says the glorious light of the Gospel of our Lord Jesus Christ shone into our blindness (Satan had blinded our eyes), woke us up, and now we are live. He said, "*. . . arise from the dead, and Christ shall give thee light.*" Not only will He give you light, He will make you light. We have read all these verses in order to read this next verse. In respect to all these things (reproving the works of darkness, walking in the light and being the light of the world, a city set on the side of the hill) He said, "*See then that ye walk circumspectly, not as fools, but as wise, Redeeming the time, because the days are evil. Wherefore be ye not unwise, but understanding what the will of the Lord is.*"

You can learn how to walk in the wisdom of God. That is what Jesus told you to do. He told you to walk in wisdom. Let's read it again. He said, "*See then that ye walk circumspectly. . .*" The word circumspectly in the Greek text means accurately. "*See then that ye walk ac-*

curately. . .'' The word actually carries even more meaning. It means accuracy which comes from being careful. Remember when you were in school and you were so careful to be accurate? In our world, where we live today, there is an accuracy which comes from being careful. God tells us through the apostle Paul to be accurate. This accuracy comes from being careful. God is saying, see then that you walk carefully so you can be accurate. God wants you to be accurate! When someone is accurate, they hit the mark. In the armed services soldiers are given a medal for accuracy on the firing range. They receive a medal for being accurate. Do you know what the literal definition for the word sin is? To miss the mark. Sin means to miss the mark. God said for us to be accurate. If you are purposing within yourself to walk accurately then you will not walk in sin. You will walk in the light instead of darkness.

"See then that you walk accurately, not as fools, but as wise, Redeeming the time. . . " Redeeming the time means making the best of the time. God said I want you to make the best of your time. You need to ask yourself, ''Am I making the best of my time?'' Why? Because the days of your life are the most valuable thing you possess. Make the best of your time since the days are evil. There is much wickedness in our world today. All around us we see evil. He says for us to make the best of our time. You must purpose to make the best of your time, for the devil will attempt to steal it. The most valuable thing you possess today is your time. It is more valuable than diamonds, more valuable than gold, more valuable than your car, more valuable than your house. It is more valuable than anything you own. You can get another

house, another coat, another bicycle. You can get another of any of those things, but you can not get another today. When this day is over, it is gone.

The fact that you are reading this book proves that you want to make the best of your time. Reading this book, though, will not do anything to regain all the hours already passed. But it will do something to make the hours ahead of you better.

I Corinthians 1:30, *"But of him are ye in Christ Jesus. . . "* Are you in Christ Jesus? Then he is talking about you. *"But of him are ye in Christ Jesus, who of God is made unto us wisdom, and righteousness, and sanctification, and redemption."* Multitudes of Christian people, without ever reading this verse, would agree if asked what they have received through the death, burial, and resurrection of the Lord Jesus. "What did He give you?" Some would say redemption. Others would say righteousness. Still others would say sanctification. But very few would say wisdom. We do not think of wisdom in terms of what Jesus purchased for us in His resurrection.

I Corinthians 2:1, *"And I, brethren, when I came to you, came not with excellency of speech or of wisdom, declaring unto you the testimony of God. For I determined not to know any thing among you, save Jesus Christ, and him crucified. And I was with you in weakness, and in fear, and in much trembling. And my speech and my preaching was not with enticing words of man's wisdom, but in demonstration of the Spirit and of power. That your faith should not stand in the wisdom of men, but in the power of God."* Where does God want your faith to stand? In the power of God. *"Howbeit we speak*

7

wisdom among them that are perfect. . . " The word perfect means "mature." *". . . yet not the wisdom of this world. . . "* He is drawing a distinction between two wisdoms. He is talking about the wisdom of this world and the wisdom of God. There are only two kinds of wisdom — the wisdom of God and the wisdom of the world. There is no middle ground. There are no other sources of information besides God and the world. *"Howbeit we speak wisdom among them that are perfect: yet not the wisdom of this world, nor of the princes of this world, that come to nought (or their end result is nothing): But we speak the wisdom of God in a mystery, even the hidden wisdom, which God ordained before the world into our glory. Which none of the princes of this world knew: for had they known it* (Known what? The wisdom that God had was hidden before the foundation of the world to bring you and me glory.) *they would not have crucified the Lord of glory."*

You and I can know things that the devil does not know. God has hidden it. That is why not everyone can read the Bible and understand it — it is written in a mystery. You need the writer of the mystery to reveal it to you. His name is the Holy Spirit.

Continuing in verse 7: *"But we speak the wisdom of God in a mystery, even the hidden wisdom, which God ordained before the world unto our glory: Which none of the princes of this world knew: for had they known it, they would not have crucified the Lord of glory. But as it is written, Eye hath not seen, nor ear heard, neither have entered into the heart of man, the things which God hath prepared for them that love him."* You cannot see the things that God has prepared for you through your eye or through your ear or through natural human means. This wisdom that God has hidden for our glory cannot be received and understood by just anyone.

Verse 10, *"But God hath revealed them unto us by his Spirit: for the Spirit searcheth all things, yea, the deep things of God. For what man knoweth the things of man, save the spirit of man which is in him. . ."* Do you see how fruitless it is to sit around and say, "I know what so-and-so is thinking." You do not. You do not have the foggiest idea what so-and-so is thinking. You do not know what is on the inside of them. *"For what man knoweth the things of man, save the spirit of man which is in him. . ."* You cannot know what someone is thinking, so do not try to figure it out.

I know people who spend their entire lives trying to figure out what other people are thinking so they can make sneaky little moves. Then when they make all their sneaky little moves the person ends up doing something else. You just don't know what people are going to do. If there is anything I have learned as a pastor, it is that you never know what people will do. You never know. Every day is a new surprise. I am not kidding. Just as soon as you think you have them figured out, they will do something to make you say, "I never thought. . ."

Verse 11, *". . . even so the things of God knoweth no man, but the Spirit of God."* The Spirit of God knows the things of God. *"Now we have received, not the spirit of the world, but the spirit which is of God. . ."* Why have we received the Spirit of God? *". . . that we might know the things that are freely given to us of God."* Verse 13, *"Which things also we speak. . ."* What are we supposed to speak? The things which the Spirit of God has shown us.

9

Let's go on. *"Which things also we speak, not in the words which man's wisdom teacheth..."* "There is human wisdom. Seeing is believing — an apple a day — cleanliness is next to godliness. This is human, natural wisdom. But the things that we speak are *"... not in the words which man's wisdom teacheth, but which the Holy Ghost teacheth; comparing spiritual things with spiritual."* Where is our vocabulary level supposed to be? On spiritual things, comparing spiritual things with spiritual.

Verse 14, *"But the natural man receiveth not the things of the Spirit of God: for they are foolishness unto him..."* What did Ephesians 5 say? *"See then ye walk accurately, not as fools, but as wise."* We are talking about receiving the wisdom of God. In I Corinthians 2:14 he says that the things of the Spirit of God (these things are the wisdom of God) are foolishness unto the natural man. Do you see that? They are foolishness to him. For you to listen to me teach the Bible is foolishness to the natural man. Why? Because it is a wisdom hidden from him. He does not have the Spirit of God in him to reveal it to him.

Do not become upset with your unsaved friends because they do not understand the Bible. They are doing the best that they can. They cannot help it if they are walking in darkness. It is our job to bring them the light so that they can get out of the darkness. For years the church has looked at the world and said, "All you people are in darkness and we're not going to have anything to do with you — not until you come over here with us." A man walked up to another man one time and said, "Jesus is the answer," and the man said, "I don't even know the question."

10

"But the natural man receiveth not the things of the Spirit of God: for they are foolishness unto him: neither can he know them, because they are spiritually discerned (or understood). *But he that is spiritual judgeth all things* (the word judgeth should be translated discerns), *yet he himself is judged of no man."*

Your relatives cannot figure you out. They will tell you, "I can't figure you out anymore. You are weird." Do not let it bother you. Just smile and say, "Thank God."

I am glad I do not walk with those guys anymore. Hallelujah! I'm glad I don't walk with them anymore. I love them and pray for them, and praise God I shoot some light at them every chance I get and watch them blink. Do you know what I'm talking about? A lot of people have lived in darkness so long they think they are in the light, that is, until you walk in with your light beaming at them. At first they cannot stand the light, but they will get used to it. One thing you do not want to do is grab the person, pull his head back, and stick the flashlight right in his eyes saying, "You are going to like this!" You do not want to do that. The Bible says that we are to be temperate in all things.

Let's go back to verse 15, *"But he that is spiritual judgeth all things, yet he himself is judged (or discerned) of no man. For who hath known the mind of the Lord, that he may instruct him. . . "* In other words, who can teach God? *"For who hath known the mind of the Lord, that he may instruct him? But we have the mind of Christ."* This does not mean that you have the same

11

mental capabilities that Christ has to know all things and remember all things. What He does mean is that we know His mind, His thoughts, and His will for our lives. That is not what it says. For some reason people read this and think they have become superbrains. Read it in context. *"For who hath known the mind of the Lord, that he may instruct him."* In other words, who knows so much about what God is doing that he can give Him instructions? None of us know the mind of God concerning the world, do we? We do not know what He is doing or what His plans are. We know very little of what God wants to do. God has given us the responsibility to win our cities to Jesus Christ, but I would not begin to say that we have all of God's understanding concerning how it will be done. We do not have His mind so that we can instruct Him, but we do have the mind of Christ. His knowledge has been given to us in certain areas to enable us to know the wisdom of God.

Let's go on. I Corinthians 3:1, *"And I, brethren, could not speak unto you as unto spiritual (or unto wise) but as unto carnal, even as unto babes in Christ."* Remember in Chapter 2 verse 6 he said the wisdom of God is spoken to them that are perfect or mature. Now he compares maturity and babes. *"I have fed you with milk..."* Can you believe that? Everything we read in the previous verses Paul called milk. That's milk? What is meat? If he calls I Corinthians 13 milk, what is meat? If he called Chapters 11 and 12 milk (where he talks about the gifts of the Spirit), then what is meat? And if that is milk, where do you think people are who do not believe the gifts of the Spirit are for today? If people say

12

they are not of God then they have no possibility of growing since Peter said they were milk. If you are not growing then you are dying. In any area of your life — if you are not growing then you are dying. *"I have fed you with milk, and not with meat: for hitherto ye were not able to bear it, neither yet now are ye able."* Why can't they bear the meat of the Word? *"For ye are yet carnal. . ."* Now he defines carnal for you. *". . . for whereas there is among you envying, and strife, and divisions, are ye not carnal, and walk as men?"* The Greek text says *"walk as mere unchanged men."* And if you are unchanged then you are still walking as foolish people in the world. That is what strife and division will do for you. It will take you back to where you once were.

We are talking about walking in wisdom. James 3:13, *"Who is a wise man and endued with knowledge among you? let him shew out of a good conversation. . ."* The word conversation should be translated behavior. *". . . let him shew out of a good behaviour. . ."* Do you remember what Paul wrote in Ephesians 5? This all ties together.

Ephesians 5:3, *"But fornication, and all uncleanness, or covetousness, let it not be once named among you, as becometh saints; Neither filthiness, nor foolish talking, nor jesting, which are not convenient: but rather giving of thanks. For this ye know, that no whoremonger, nor unclean person, nor covetous man, who is an idolater, hath any inheritance in the kingdom of Christ and of God."* Verse 11, *"And have no fellowship with the unfruitful works of darkness, but rather reprove them."* What did Jesus say in Matthew 5 about works? That our good works glorify the Father and

13

through our good works we let out light shine. Do you see how it all fits together? Our actions and our deeds speak very loudly. I love to look at things like this.

James 3:13 says, "*. . . let him shew out of a good behaviour his works with meekness of wisdom.*" Wisdom produces meekness. We have a poor image in the Body of Christ today about meekness. W. E. Vine said meekness is the hardest word in the New Testament to define. Let me give you an illustration of what meekness is. The book of Numbers, the seventh chapter, says that Moses was the meekest man in the whole earth. That is not a characteristic we generally attribute to Moses, is it? When you think of Moses you think of someone bold and brash, full of faith, confidence, wisdom, ability, and knowledge. I wonder how many people would think of meekness when describing Moses? But the Bible says he was the meekest man in all the earth. Jesus said the meek would inherit the earth.

One definition of meekness is knowing that God will stand behind your words. Another definition of meekness is that you do not have to push yourself on other people to prove you are right. The next verse will further prove this definition. Verse 14, "*But if ye have bitter envying and strife in your hearts. . .*" That word strife in the Greek text means the desire to seek followers to cause division. "*But if ye have bitter envying and the desire to seek followers to cause division, glory not, and lie not against the truth. This wisdom descendeth not from above, but is earthly, sensual, devilish.*" There is a truth revealed in these verses that you must learn.

It is vital that you walk in wisdom, knowing what the wisdom of God is, because there is a false wisdom in the earth that Satan will use to deceive you. In Genesis chapter 3 Satan deceived Eve, making her think that by partaking of the tree of the knowledge of good and evil she would become wise. Satan will try to make you think that his lies are actually the wisdom of God. "Well, I'll tell you this, Charles, I know there is something bad going on at my job. God has shown me that it is my responsibility to tell the rest of the people on the job what my boss is doing wrong. I'm going to tell everyone because God has told me to do it." You are wrong. You have been lied to. You are partaking of the tree of the knowledge of good and evil instead of the tree of life, which is the wisdom of God. You are seeking followers to cause division. That wisdom is from the earth and it is sensual and devilish and deceptive. That is very strong, isn't it? Do not fall into that trap.

I am warning you to not get in strife on your job, in your neighborhood, with your government, in your church, in your family, etc. If someone comes along with a wisdom trying to seek followers to cause division, you need to put distance between you and them, because that wisdom does not come from God. I do not care if they sugar coat it with, "I was praying and God revealed this to me." Do not listen! The Bible says that wisdom is from hell, but people still call it wisdom.

I have had people call me on the phone and say, "Charles, I believe the Lord has shown me this about a situation on my job. I think I ought to get the rest of the people in my office together to talk about it. What do you think?" I tell them not to. The desire to seek followers to cause division does not ascend from above. It is earthly, sensual, and devilish. "What should I do?" Go

15

to the man himself, the way the Bible tells you to. Better yet, get on your face before God and pray. If he is wrong God will change him. If he is not wrong He will change you.

The main problem that we have in our country is too many fault-finders. Too many people want to find something wrong and then talk about it. Yes, our nation has problems, but not everything in America is bad and corrupt. There are a lot of good things happening in our nation. There are a lot of good people in our nation. It is time for us to band together to overcome the problems. Seeking followers to cause division, in the name of making our country better, is actually working to destroy our country. Do not listen to that garbage. *"But the wisdom that is from above is first pure. . . "* If your wisdom is not pure then you need to get a different wisdom. The wisdom of God is peaceable. If the wisdom coming out of your mouth does not produce peace, if it produces division, then it is not of God. There are times when I have to keep my mouth shut, because I would enjoy stirring up some strife. Have you ever been in that position? I have been there more times than I care to think about. Sometimes you must grit your teeth. The psalmist David said he put a hand over his mouth when the evil one was before him. He asked God to put a bridle in his mouth so he would not sin against the Lord.

The wisdom of God is gentle. It is easy to be intreated. You do not have to have fourteen doctorate degrees to understand the Bible. Anyone can understand God's wisdom. God's wisdom is full of mercy and good fruits, and is without partiality. If you have a revelation from God, and it is not for everybody, then you did not get it from God. If your revelation must be preceded with, "Now, don't tell anybody I told you this," you better not say it. God's wisdom is without partiality and without hypocrisy. It says the same thing, no matter who reads it. The Word of God reads the same regardless of what your background is, who you are, what side of town you live on, what color you are, or how much money you make. The Word of God reads the same to every person who reads it — doesn't it? It is without hypocrisy. It does not read one way to the rich man, and another way to the poor man. It reads the same to everyone. That is the wisdom of God.

Chapter II

THE KEY TO UNDERSTANDING WISDOM

Ephesians 5:6, *"Let no man deceive you with vain words: for because of these things cometh the wrath of God upon the children of disobedience. Be not ye therefore partakers with them. For ye were sometimes darkness. . . "* We discussed this in the last chapter but I want us to go over it again. He did not say that you walked in darkness sometimes, although we all did. Paul said that you were sometimes darkness. He did not say you were once in darkness, although you were. He said you once were darkness. Then he goes on to say that now you are light. Jesus said the same thing in Matthew, the fifth chapter. He said that you are the light of the world. That is somewhat difficult to accept. We find it hard to say that about ourselves. But Jesus said it, and if He said it then it must be the truth.

"But Charles, I don't feel like the light." How do

you know what light feels like? You cannot base the truth-fulness of God's Word on your feelings. If you do not learn anything else by reading this book, learn this — you cannot base the reality of God's Word on your feelings. You are not to believe the Word is true because you feel it is true. The Word is true regardless of your feelings. It is the final authority. Your body may say one thing and your mind something else, your relatives may speak this and your neighbor may speak that, your newspaper may proclaim certain statements and your boss others. People can say what they think, but when God speaks, His Word is the final authority. God does not really care what we think about it. His Word is the final authority. That is the way you have to approach it.

If you are going to grow, you must believe the Word is the final authority. If you do not receive this truth, I can assure you that you will not grow. You will compromise, you will back down, you will give up, you will throw in the towel, you will quit, you will faint and lose courage. Either you make the decision in your heart that the Word is the final authority or you will be overcome.

The Word which is the final authority says you are light in the Lord. You are to walk as children of the light. *"For the fruit of the Spirit is in all goodness and righteousness and truth; Proving what is acceptable unto the Lord."* When you walk as children of the light you will prove what is acceptable unto the Lord. Paul said in Romans the 12th chapter that when you have your mind renewed to the Word you will prove the will of God in your life. In Ephesians 5 he said for us to walk in the light and walk as children of light, that we may prove what is acceptable unto the Lord. We can take those two scriptures and put them together to say that a part of walking in the light is to have your mind renewed to the Word of God.

All of us have had false information put into our brains — information that is contrary to what we read in the Bible. Have you discovered that to be true? I have. We have false information in our minds. Information that is not the truth. It may be true, but it is not the truth. There is a difference. It may be true that you are sick, but the truth says by the stripes of Jesus you are healed. Do you understand that? Do you see the difference? We do not deny that something is true, but we can change it with the truth.

Let's continue reading. "*And have no fellowship with the unfruitful works* (What is fellowship? Fellowship is common interests and common desires) *of darkness, but rather reprove them. For it is a shame even to speak of those things which are done of them in secret. But all things that are reproved are made manifest by the light. . .*" Who is the light? We are the light. What does the light do? It reproves and makes manifest.

"*. . .for whatsoever doth make manifest is light. Wherefore he saith, Awake thou that sleepest, and arise from the dead, and Christ shall give thee light. See then that ye walk circumspectly. . .*" The word circumspectly means accuracy which comes from being careful. Paul says for us to walk accurately. He is not telling us to be full of worry. He is not telling us to be full of fear. He said be careful. If you are careful how you walk, you will walk accurately.

Now remember, Jesus said that the way we walk is narrow. Straight is the path and narrow is the way. Have you ever walked on something that was very narrow? You have to be careful, don't you? You must be careful how you walk because there is darkness all around us. When you are careful how you walk, then you will be accurate. God wants you to be accurate. If you are accurate, then you will not miss the mark. The literal definition of the word sin is to miss the mark. I do not want to sin — do you? I want to be perfect in my walk.

"Oh, but Charles, nobody can do that." Maybe not, but I can still try. I would rather try for 100% and only get 70% than try for 50% and only get 25%. It takes more effort to go for 100%, but if you are going to run the race then you might as well run it right. If you are going to live by faith, then do it right. If we are going to walk in the light, then let's walk in the light. If we are going to live this life, then let's do it right. That is what he is saying to us. He is saying walk carefully, walk accurately, do not miss the mark. Then, he tells us how to do it.

Verse 15, "*See then that ye walk circumspectly* (accurately), *not as fools, but as wise, Redeeming the time. . .*" The word redeeming means making the best of the time. Why do we need to make the best of the time? Because the days are evil. You do not have to look very far to agree with that. We live in evil days. There is wickedness around us. Do not let your heart become overcharged and overloaded with the wickedness causing you to become discouraged and say, "Oh my Lord, the times are so bad and so wicked. These days are so terrible and so ugly. I wish I had not been born now. I wish I was not alive now. I wish this and I wish that."

There really is not much more happening today than

there was 20 years ago. It is just that today evil gets more publicity. Men were running around on their wives twenty years ago. People were getting drunk and addicted to drugs twenty years ago. People were under tremendous pressure twenty years ago. These are the good old days. Quit wishing you could go back in time because you cannot. You cannot go back to Mickey Mouse and Peter Pan. You are a big boy or big girl now and you have responsibilities. There are things God requires of you. The more you learn from His Word, the more He requires of you.

He says walk accurately, *". . . not as fools, but as wise, Redeeming* (making the best of) *the time, because the days are evil. Wherefore be ye not unwise. . . "* The Charles Nieman translation says next, *"Therefore be ye not a dummy. . ., but understanding what the will of the Lord is."* This is an interesting thought. With it we are going to pop some religious balloons. The first thing we need to understand is God desires that you know His will for your life. Now that shocks people, that amazes people, that astounds people. Most people think that God wants us to live in darkness. He does not want you live in darkness! Praise God, He redeemed you from the darkness! God does not want you to live in darkness. He sent His Son so that the people who lived in darkness could see the great light and come out of darkness. That is why He came — to get you out of darkness. God does not want you to be ignorant of His will. He wants you to understand His will.

Let us read it again. Verse 17, *"Wherefore be ye not unwise, but understanding what the will of the Lord is."* The dictionary defines wisdom as "the quality or state of being wise." That clears it up, doesn't it? Fortunately it goes on with the definition. Wisdom is "the knowledge of what is true or right coupled with good judgment."

There is a difference between wisdom and knowledge. There are a lot of people, college graduates, with a head full of knowledge. Many times they are educated beyond their intellects. You probably know some. I do. Their brain has been embalmed with knowledge, but they have not the slightest idea what to do with it. Just gaining knowledge is not the key. Now God does not place a premium on ignorance. God does not look around and say, "I want the dumbest person I can find and I will use him." That is not how He thinks. God does not place a premium on ignorance.

There is more to walking in the Kingdom of God than gaining knowledge of Bible principles, memorizing scripture or having a mental understanding of spiritual realities and laws. There are people who can explain to you the doctrine of the new birth, but they are not born-again themselves. There are many tremendous messages preached from the Bible every Sunday by people who do not have any idea what it says. The message sounds good, looks good, feels good, and even tastes good. But ask them, "How do I get out of troubles?" and they will say, "I don't know, read your Bible and pray." That statement is used by the ministry just as, "Take two aspirins and call me in the morning," is used by the medical profession.

You need to read your Bible and pray — no doubt about that. But sometimes you have to be shown how, don't you? Praise God, this is a "how to" book. The Bible is not a "don't" book. It is a "how to" book. Quit thinking of the Bible as a "don't" book and start thinking of it as a "how to" book. The Bible tells you how to live, how to be healed, and how to walk in the wisdom of God.

What is wisdom? It is the knowledge of what is true or right, coupled with good judgment. So we could say that wisdom is the ability to use knowledge. The dictionary defines wise as meaning "having the power of discerning and judging properly as to what is true or right." With God's ability to know what is true and right, coupled with good judgment and His power to discern and judge, we will come out ahead. We are talking about walking in the wisdom of God, not in the wisdom of men. I do not want to walk in the wisdom of men. Men have wisdom and God has wisdom. Most of us have been programmed with men's wisdom, some of which was not wrong. Not everything you learned growing up was wrong. Part of it was true, but then other parts were lies. Of the lies, some were subtle, a perversion of the truth.

Proverbs 4:20-22, *"My son, attend to my words; incline thine ear unto my sayings. Let them not depart from thine eyes; keep them in the midst of thine heart. For they are life unto those that find them, and health to all their flesh."* If you do what these verses say, the Word will be life to you and medicine to your flesh. If you put God's Word before your eyes, listen to it, and keep it in your heart, it will be life to you and medicine to your flesh. If you are not experiencing the life of God and health in your body then ask yourself, "Am I attending unto the Word? Am I hearing God's Word? Am I hearing what God says?" Attending and hearing means more than reading a few verses just before you go to bed at night or listening to a tape as you go to sleep. Those things are good, but you need to be doing more with the Word than that.

Are you attending unto the Word? He said put it before your eyes. Are you spending time reading it? Do you have it before your eyes? If not, then start. Do you have it in your heart? How do you put God's Word into your heart? By choosing to believe it. Believing is a choice, a decision, not a feeling. Sometimes I do not feel like believing the Word, but I choose to believe it anyway. "Why Charles?" Because I know what it will do for me.

Proverbs 4:1, *"Hear, ye children, the instruction of a father, and attend to know understanding. For I give you good doctrine, forsake ye not my law. For I was my father's son, tender and only beloved in the sight of my mother. He taught me also, and said unto me, Let thine heart retain my words: keep my commandments, and live. Get wisdom . . ."*

What are you supposed to get? Wisdom. What is wisdom? The quality or state of being wise, the knowledge of what is true or right, coupled with good judgment. He said get wisdom — get wisdom into your life. Obtain the knowledge of what is true and right. The only way you are going to obtain the knowledge of what is true and right is to spend time in the Word.

There are a lot of things in the world which appear to be true and right, but they are not. In addition, not everything in the world is wrong. Some of it is right. "How am I going to know the difference?" Think. How about that for an answer? I am serious — use the brain God gave you. Think about your life. Think about what you are doing. Think about what is happening in your life. Think about it. Think about what you hear and then compare it with what you read in God's Word. If what you hear does not agree with what you read, then make what you hear agree with what you read. Take God's Word and exalt it in your life, instead of what people are saying.

All around us there are opportunities to fail, opportunities to go under. But I am more convinced than ever that if the church of Jesus Christ will take God's Word and stand upon it, then the church will come to the forefront. Many people now at the front are running to the rear because of fear. As God releases the revival He has planned for the earth, the church will be at the front and the sinners at the back, wondering what happened.

It will take courage and you will have to walk in the wisdom of God to accomplish it. Life has gotten harder. This is not the time for "tweedle dee" Christians to walk through life playing games and saying, "I can't wait until I get to heaven." We need some help now. Today in your city, people are dying and going to hell and you can do something about it. "I can't, Charles, I'm not called to preach." Maybe not, but you are called to lay hands upon the sick and cast out devils and speak with new tongues. "I could never do that." Yes, you can. "Charles, you do not know." Possibly I do not, but God does and He said you can do it. If He says you can do it then you can do it. He that lives within you is going to do it through you.

Verse 5, *"Get wisdom, get understanding: forget it not* (don't forget the wisdom of God); *neither decline from the words of my mouth."* This verse tells you how to get the wisdom of God — you get wisdom from the

27

Word of God. You are not going to get wisdom anywhere else.

A famous fortune teller said she looked into the eyes of a serpent and beheld the wisdom of the ages. Bless her heart. That sounds real spiritual and there are a lot of people who believe everything she says. But the thing you must understand is that God said His wisdom comes from His Word. I am not interested in the wisdom of the serpent. I want to know the wisdom of God. The wisdom of the serpent produces death. If you do not believe me, ask Adam and Eve. They listened to his wisdom and they died.

In verse 6 He continues talking about wisdom, *"Forsake her not. . . "* Do not ever leave the wisdom of God. When you start walking in the wisdom of God, just keep right on going, never plan on quitting. Make the decision that you are going to do this for the rest of your life. I will show you why you will want to do this. *"Forsake her not, and she shall preserve thee. . . "* When you begin to walk in wisdom, instead of walking in foolishness, the wisdom of God will preserve you. The word preserve literally defined means *"to keep alive or in existence, to make lasting, to keep safe from harm or injury."*

God's wisdom will do that for you. God's wisdom will perserve you. It will keep you alive and in existence. It will make you last. And — I like this — it will keep you safe from harm or injury. Do you know why? Because you will be walking in the light. When you are walking in the light you can see what the devil is trying to do to you and you can walk around it, over it, or knock it out of the way. The only time you get hurt is when you are walking in

28

darkness. You cannot see what is in front of you so you stumble. But what I am telling you is that Satan will purposefully try to get you into darkness. He will throw things in your path because he knows you cannot see them when you are in the dark. But when you are walking in the light you will be kept safe.

Verse 6, *". . . love her. . ."* God said love wisdom. *". . . and she shall keep thee.* Wisdom is the principal thing. . ."* The word principal means "first or highest as in rank, importance or value." God tells you to make wisdom the first thing in your life — the highest thing in your life — the thing that ranks the highest — the most important thing in your life. He puts a lot of emphasis on wisdom, doesn't He? He instructs you and me to make the wisdom of God first in importance in our lives. This is not a suggestion. He said for us to make the wisdom of God the first thing in our life. In your life there are all kinds of things that have rank. Rank has its privileges. The things you rank highest in your life get the most attention — they have more privilege. Isn t that right? You give them more attention. We are told to rank wisdom first, because wisdom is the principal thing.

Jesus revealed this to Mary and Martha. When He came to their house Mary chose to sit at His feet and hear His Word, while Martha went into the kitchen to fix Him something to eat. Fix Him something to eat. Jesus, who just a few days before took five loaves and two fishes and fed 15,000 people! She eventually became very upset at Mary and Jesus. I want you to picture this. Jesus is in the room teaching, speaking the words of life. While He is teaching Martha is in the kitchen trying to cook. What was first place in her life? Food. What was first in Mary's life? The Word. Martha finally came out of the kitchen and interrupted Jesus while He was teaching. Can you imagine that? The Messiah was sitting in her living room teaching and she came in saying, "Lord, don't you care that my sister is sitting here doing nothing and I'm in there slaving over that hot stove?" That is a pretty loose translation but it will work for the point of illustration. Jesus looked at her and said, "Martha, you are right. Mary, you lazy thing, you get up and help your sister." No, He did not say that. He looked at Martha and said, "Martha, you are careful and troubled about many things." It was not only the food that had her upset. There were many things in her life and heart which had her troubled and upset, keeping her from getting into the Word. The meal was just an excuse. If it had not been that it would have been something else. She was troubled about many things. She had allowed care, worry, and anxiety about the age in which she lived to overwhelm her heart. Jesus looked at her and said, "Martha, you are troubled about many things, but Mary has chosen that good part." What part did she choose? To sit at the feet of Jesus to hear the Word. He said, "Mary has chosen that good part and it shall not be taken from her." What Mary had chosen would be her's eternally.

That tells us something about God s Word. When the Word comes into your heart it lodges in your spirit. It takes root in you. If you believe it and hold onto it, the devil cannot take it away from you. It will be yours forever. What you spend time looking at and listening to is what you will depend upon when you get in trouble. If you spend all your time looking at and listening to soap operas, you will have nothing to draw upon when trouble comes.

He said, *"Wisdom is the principle thing; therefore get wisdom . . ."* God desires that you make wisdom number one in your life. He said to get wisdom and with your getting get understanding. Get the wisdom of God and then understand it.

Verse 8, *"Exalt her . . ."* The word exalt means "elevate in rank, honor, power, character and quality." Elevate the wisdom of God. If His wisdom is not first in your life, then elevate it. Elevate it in rank, elevate it in honor, elevate it in power, elevate it in your life. Bring that Word up into your life. He said to elevate wisdom, and then wisdom shall promote you.

If you had a choice between being promoted and failing which one would you take? God wants to promote you. The word promote means "to encourage the existence or progress of, to further, to advance in rank." It will advance you in rank, dignity, and position. It will do that for you.

That is what happened to David. David sat in the field tending sheep. At night he could look up into the heavens and see the glory of God. At times he would begin to sing about the glory of God. The Holy Spirit would rise up in David's heart and he began to sing of things he had no knowledge of. God's wisdom became his as a young boy. One day while Samuel was praying, God spoke to him and told him to go to Judah to anoint a king. Now human reasoning would have said — "Why? We already have a king named Saul." If anyone ever looked like a king, Saul did. The Bible says he was head and shoulders above any man in Israel. That means he stood somewhere in the area of seven feet tall.

31

But God said, "I want you to go to Judah and anoint a king." So Samuel — his job is to obey, not to figure out — went to Judah and eventually found Jesse's house. He told Jesse he wanted to see his sons. Jesse brought in six of them — the oldest to the youngest, except one. Samuel began with the oldest. Human wisdom would reason that if there was a king in that house, he would be the oldest. That was the way it was done in the nation of Israel. The oldest son got everything and the youngest got what was left. Samuel looked at that first born; then the next, and then the next, all the way down to the last one, but did not find a king.

Remember, this is the prophet Samuel. In the nation of Israel, a prophet whose prophecies did not come to pass was stoned to death. The pressure was on Samuel. Human wisdom would have said, "Anoint one of the boys. Anything is better than being stoned." But he turned to Jesse and asked him if he had another son. Jesse replied, "Yes, David, but he is young, with a ruddy complexion, and is only 17 years old." Samuel told Jesse to get him.

So they brought David in. Now here is the boy who has been sitting out in the field. Nobody knew who he was. Nobody had ever heard of him or knew anything about him, but he had the wisdom of God. God's wisdom was dwelling inside of him. He had made God's Word and God's ways of doing things his ways of doing things. The moment Samuel saw him the Spirit of God revealed to him that David was the king of Israel. Samuel poured the anointing oil upon David to anoint him as king of Israel.

A few days later we see David encountering Goliath. Goliath stood in a valley three times a day cursing Saul, the nation of Israel, and their God. Saul, the king, moved his tent to the back of the lines! The nation of Israel — God's chosen people — were so afraid of this one man that they dug holes in the ground and lived in them like dogs. A 17 year old boy came to them, with the wisdom of God, and asked them if there was no longer a God in Israel. "Who is this uncircumcised Philistine dog?" They looked at David and said, "we know the naughtiness of your heart." Do you know what they were saying to him? The same thing they are saying about you. "Well, don't you think you are something now that you have yourself a little Bible and little religion in your life. We know what a big shot you think you are." Just blow them off, ignore them, don't listen to them. David looked at them and said, "He's just like the lion and the bear." He had already killed a lion and a bear when they came after his sheep.

"But Charles, that was David." Who do you think you are? The Bible says now we are the sons of God. A 17 year old boy said, "I will cut his head off." They snapped back, "You are going home!" David's very thoughts and actions reproved them, just as you reprove people since you are light. Finally Saul heard about him. Saul knew the anointing and wisdom of God when he saw it. Saul told David, "I believe you can do it." David replied, "I will cut his head off. I will feed his carcass to the fowls of the air and the beasts of the field!" Saul then gave David his armor. Can you imagine David putting on Saul's armor? Saul was about seven feet tall and David was still a boy. David finally evaded Saul's offer by stating that he hadn't tested the armor. David said, "I have my staff and my sling."

Goliath was approximately 9 feet tall and weighed in the area of 300 to 400 pounds. He was not somebody you played games with. When David shouted to him, "I'm going to cut your head off!" Goliath started laughing and said, "Am I a dog that you send a child out to me?" David quit talking. I love this part. The Bible says he started running at Goliath. The world would say that this was not very smart. This man was 9 feet tall, He could rip your arms off and beat you over the head with them. As David ran toward Goliath he stopped at a brook to pick up five smooth stones. Some people reason that he picked up five stones because he was afraid he would miss the first shot. If you study the Bible you will discover that he picked up five stones because Golaith had four brothers. David planned on getting rid of all five of them that day.

This is a 17 year old boy — a shepherd with no education. He did not have the written Bible as you have. All he knew was what God had shown him when he was sitting out in those fields. And he had the courage to believe it. He came running down the hill, picked up five smooth stones, and ran to where Goliath was yelling at him. The Bible says that David had no sword in his hand. Do you know why? Because he had one in his mouth! The Word of God! He ran at Goliath shouting, "I'm going to cut your head off!" When Goliath raised his head back to laugh, David sunk a stone into the side of his head. Goliath fell over. David then climbed up on his chest, pulled out his sword, cut off Goliath's head, and held it up. The Bible says there was a victory shout in the camp of Israel. They all ran after and killed the Philistines, gaining a great victory that day. Why? Because a 17 year old boy, who was at the very back of the class, reached out and embraced the wisdom of God.

Proverbs 4:8 tells us to embrace wisdom. The word embrace means "to take and clasp in your arms, press to your bosom, to take or receive gladly or eagerly, accept willingly, to avail yourself, to adopt, to take into the eye of the mind, to encircle, surround and enclose."

David embraced the wisdom of God. When he did this it promoted him. It advanced him from the shepherd boy to king of Israel. The wisdom of God. That wisdom belongs to you. You can have it.

Jesus compared a wise man and foolish man in Matthew 7:21-27. He said that a wise man is a man who hears His words and does them. He said the man who hears His words and does them is likened into a man which built his house upon a rock. When the floods came and the winds blew and the rains fell, his house stood because it was founded upon the rock. We are living in that time now. The wind is blowing, the rain is falling, the storm has come. We are in it. Then he said that a foolish man is one who hears His Word and does not do it. He is likened unto a man who built his house upon sand. When the winds blew and the rains fell and the floods came, the house fell.

So what is the key to walking in the wisdom of God? Being a doer of God's Word! When you read it, do it. You should write this next statement down and read it every day. "God said it and I believe it and that settles it."

Wisdom will promote you. Wisdom will bring you

to honor. Proverbs 4:9, *"She shall give to thine head an ornament of grace: a crown of glory shall she deliver to thee. Hear, O my son, and receive my sayings; and the years of thy life shall be many."* That is better than the years of your life being few, If you hear His Word and do it, then you are wise. If you hear His Word and don't do it, then you are foolish. "But Charles, what if I don't want to do it?" Well, that is your decision. Nobody can make that decision for you. But I would hope that after you read these things you would choose to be preserved and kept and promoted to receive an ornament of grace and a crown of glory, living a long life. You must make wisdom the principal thing. You must rank it, if need be, above sleep for the rest of your life. If the only time that you can get into the Word is early in the morning, then get up early. If the only time that you can get into the Word is late at night, then stay up late. But whatever you have to do to get in the Word, do it. Get that wisdom. Get yourself a tape recorder and carry it with you from room to room. Whatever you need to do in your life, do it. "Forsake wisdom not."

Chapter III

APPLYING GOD'S WISDOM IN YOUR LIFE

In Proverbs 4:1, Solomon spoke to us about wisdom. *"Hear, ye children, the instruction of a father, and attend to know understanding. For I give you good doctrine, forsake ye not my law. For I was my father's son, tender and only beloved in the sight of my mother. He taught me also, and said unto me, Let thine heart retain my words: keep my commandments, and live. Get wisdom . . ."*

This is a strong statement. He is telling us to get something, and the thing he tells us to get is wisdom. He does not tell us to get religion. He said, *"Get wisdom, get understanding: forget it not; neither decline from the words of my mouth. Forsake her not, and she shall preserve thee . . ."*

Once again the word preserve means "to keep alive or in existence, to make lasting, to keep safe from harm or injury." Wisdom will preserve you. Wisdom will keep you alive and in existence. It will keep you safe from harm or injury. Wisdom will do that for you.

Now do you understand why Solomon said to get wisdom? Why would he want you to get wisdom? Wisdom produces life. It will keep you safe from harm or injury. Let's read it again, *"Get wisdom, get understanding: forget it not; neither decline from the words of my mouth. Forsake her not, and she shall preserve thee: love her, and she shall keep thee."* When you understand what wisdom will do for you, then you will see why Solomon made the statement he did in verse 7. He said that wisdom is the principal thing. Principal means "first in importance, first or highest, as in rank or in value." He said to make wisdom first in our lives. He said it is the principal thing. It ranks first. It is important.

Let's continue reading. *"Wisdom is the principal thing; therefore get wisdom and with all thy getting get understanding."* Wisdom is the knowledge of what is true or right, coupled with good judgment. The dictionary says that a wise person is one who has the power of discerning and judging properly as to what is true or right. A wise person possesses discernment. Through wisdom you have the power of discerning and judging properly as to what is true or right.

If we stopped here we could build a very strong case as to why it is important to obtain the wisdom of God. There are a number of things around us today that look good, sound good, and might even be good. But, if we do not understand and walk in the wisdom of God, we could be led astray. We could end up in trouble. There is a lot of candy-coated deception in the earth today — a lot of things that look good, sound good, and may even appear to be good, but in reality they bring destruction. In reality, they will cause you to fall. In the end they will destroy your life. There are some things that are obviously wrong when you first look at them. To some people, heroin looks good, but the rest of us know it is destructive; this is obvious, and we can see through it. But there are many subtle deceptions in this age we are living.

We need to know the wisdom of God. We need to be able to tap into God's wisdom, having the ability to discern what is true and right, as opposed to what is a lie and wrong. God is not deceived. He is not misled by false appearances. Satan will mislead you by false appearances. He will try to persuade you that something is different from the way it really is.

Isn't that what Satan did to Eve in the garden? The thing that was true and right was that, if they ate of the tree of the knowledge of good and evil, they would die. The devil said, *"No, you won't die, you will be smarter."* Eve was deceived, she was misled by a false appearance. The same thing happens today.

Proverbs 4:7, *"Wisdom is the principal thing: therefore get wisdom: and with all thy getting get understanding. Exalt her . . . "* The word exalt means "elevate in rank, honor, power, character and quality." That is what God says to do with wisdom. What value do you place on the wisdom of God in your life? "Charles, I place a tremendous value on it, I want it." Good. The next question is, what are you doing to get it? "Well, I'm not really doing anything, I just want it. Isn't that enough?" No. Just wanting to eat is not enough. Just wanting wisdom is not enough. You have to study the Word to attain it.

What are you doing to get the wisdom of God? What did Solomon say to do to obtain wisdom? Exalt her. Exalt wisdom. Elevate wisdom in honor, and in power in your life. "Charles, wisdom has power?" Yes, a part of walking in the wisdom of God is telling your spirit, your soul, and your body that the Word is true, that it has power over your decisions in spite of what you think, feel, hear, taste, or smell.

Does God's wisdom have that kind of power in your life? Is it the final authority? Is what God said about life the final authority? Only you can answer those questions. Is His Word the final authority or do you overrule it when you think it will be too hard on you or when you don't feel like acting upon it? "I'm too tired today. The problem is too big."

If you will elevate wisdom in rank, power, character, quality, and honor in your life, it will promote you. Do you know what the word promote means? It means "to advance in rank, dignity, or position." God is saying, if you will promote, if you will exalt, if you will elevate wisdom, then the wisdom that you have elevated will promote you. Compare these definitions. The word exalt means "to elevate in rank, power, honor, character, and quality," and the word promote means "to advance in rank, dignity, or position. They sound alike, do they not? So the Word tells us that whatever we do with wisdom, wisdom will do with us!

"I've never heard anything like that." Yes, you have. Jesus said the way you measure something out is the way it will be measured back to you. Do you understand that?

If you give God's wisdom the proper place in your life, if you exalt it, it will exalt you. You will rise to the same level that you place wisdom in your life. On a scale of one to ten, if you put wisdom at two, then you are going to rise only to a two. I would rather be an eleven — wouldn't you? "Charles, you always talk about going for the best." Why not? If you are going to run the race, then you might as well run to obtain the prize. (1 Corinthians 9:24)

"Exalt her (wisdom), and she (wisdom) will promote thee: she shall bring thee to honour, when thou dost embrace her." The word embrace means "to take or clasp in the arms, to press to the bosom, to take or receive gladly or eagerly." He is talking about you. We are talking about seeing your life elevated, made better, increased, lifted up in dignity through the wisdom of God — in spite of your abundance or lack of education, in spite of where you live or don't live. God's wisdom will lift you up.

"How can I be sure it will work for me?" Because Jesus said it was easier for heaven and earth to pass away than for one part of His Word to fail. That is how sure God is of His Word.

I want to share an important truth with you at this point. You do not have to understand all of God's Word in order for it to work for you. You need to act upon what you have knowledge of. Do not attempt to tell God how to answer your prayers. Your vision is very limited, but God sees the whole picture.

Examples of this can be found when people are praying for their families. It is amazing how many schemes people come up with to get their families saved. People have said to me, "Charles, do not tell my family that I asked you to do this, but do you think that you could stop by their house tonight on your way home? Do not tell them that I asked you to do it. I know that if you stopped by they would get saved." I ask them, "Do they want me to come by?" "Oh, no, they don't believe anything that you teach." "Charles, people don't do that." Yes, they do. I know they are concerned for their loved ones, but trying to fool them will not get them saved. It sounds good, but it is a deception. I have had people with a seriously ill relative in the hospital ask me to go to the hospital to pray for them. Oftentimes they will say, "Charles, I believe God will heal my uncle, and through that miracle my family will be won." That sounds good doesn't it? Do not pray that way. Why not? Because that is not the reason God will heal your uncle. The reason God will heal your uncle is that he has a right to be healed whether your family gets saved or not.

He said that if you will exalt wisdom, then wisdom will promote you. Wisdom will bring you to honor when you gladly and eagerly embrace her. Have you ever noticed how excited children get about Christmas? They cannot wait for Christmas to come, can they? We need to have the same kind of attitude concerning God's Word. He wants us to have that same attitude towards His wisdom — to receive it gladly and eargerly, to embrace it, to accept it willingly. The word embrace also means "to avail yourself of, to adopt, to take in with the eye or the mind." What does "to take in with the eye or the mind" mean? Have you ever been walking in a shopping mall, minding your own business, not really looking for anything in particular? Suddenly, you happen to see something you cannot live another day without; you stand there and look at it. What are you doing? You are embracing that thing with your eyes and with your mind. You are receiving it eagerly into your life. Even though it is not in your hands at that moment, you are receiving it. I'm using these illustrations in order to give you an idea of what God says about His Word. His Word is His wisdom.

Let's continue on. *"She shall give to thine head an ornament of grace: a crown of glory shall she deliver to thee. Hear, O my son, and receive my sayings; and the years of thy life shall be many. I have taught thee in the way of wisdom; I have led thee in right paths. When thou goest, they steps shall not be straitened (or hindered); and when thou runnest, thou shalt not stumble. Take fast hold of instruction . . ."*

This is Solomon talking — the richest and wisest man who ever lived. He said to take fast hold of instruction and not let it go. Grip it firmly and hold on. If you fell off a boat and someone threw a rope to you, you would not let go of that rope for anything, would you? That is what he is saying. He said to take fast hold of instruction. *"Take fast hold of instruction; let her not go: keep her; for she is thy life."* Wisdom is your life! Wisdom will preserve you and keep you alive.

God's Word is God's wisdom. You cannot have God's wisdom apart from His Word. In addition, you need to learn how to listen to your spirit. Let me explain that to you. You are more than flesh and bone. You are a spirit. You have a soul and you live in a body, but you are a spirit being. It is your spirit man that is alive on the inside of your body. As you read this book, I am talking to your spirit. I believe this knowledge is going directly into your spirit, because once it gets there, it does not leave. If it goes into your head, you might forget it. You cannot depend upon your memory to retain all this knowledge. I am not talking to your mind. I am talking to your spirit man. Concentrate on what you are reading. I want you to think about what the Word says. If you will do what God's Word says, they you will walk in wisdom.

Proverbs 1:1, "The proverbs of Solomon the son of David, king of Israel; To know wisdom and instruction. . ." That is the reason the proverbs were given to us. They were given so that we can know wisdom and instruction. Why are the Proverbs given? To receive the instruction of wisdom. So we can say that wisdom begins in this book of Proverbs. Some may say, "Charles, Proverbs is an Old Testament Book." Yes, it is, but wisdom is for all ages. "To receive the instruction of wisdom, justice, and judgment, and equity; To give subtilty to the simple, to the young man knowledge and discretion. A wise man will hear. . ." How do you receive the wisdom of God? You start by hearing. Open your ears and hear what God is saying. "A wise man will hear. . ." I tell my congregation that they should purchase a tape recorder, put it in their car, and listen to teaching tapes instead of rock music or country western music. They need to listen to the wisdom of God. "But people will think I'm weird." They may for a period of time, but when they see your life improve, then they will change their attitude. When you are enjoying the abundant life and they are barely getting by, they will no longer think you are weird. They will want to know what you know.

"*A wise man will hear, and will increase learn-*

ing. . . " When you hear what God says, it cannot help but increase your learning and understanding. I have heard people say, "If I put a tape on in the house, I will be walking around and will not hear all of it." But you will hear parts of it, and any part you hear will help. "Charles, I bought a set the other day and listened to them all in one day. What do you recommend now?" The same series. "But I already heard it." No, you didn't. You did not even begin to hear it. There is a difference between hearing with the ears on your head and hearing with the ears of your spirit. I am talking about hearing with the ears of your spirit. Jesus said, *"If any man has ears to hear let him hear."* He is not talking about the ears on the side of your head — He is talking about the ears of your heart.

"A wise man will hear, and will increase learning; and a man of understanding shall attain unto wise counsels." So how do you obtain wisdom? You hear it and you attain unto wise counsels. You find people who have the wisdom of God and listen to what they have to say. Get your information from people who have the Word of God working in their lives. It amazes me how many people ask someone not filled with the Holy Ghost how to become filled with the Holy Ghost. That makes about as much sense as asking a Chevrolet dealer about an Oldsmobile. If you want to know about the Holy Ghost, ask the people who are filled with the Holy Ghost.

Proverbs 3:5, *"Trust in the Lord with all thine heart; and lean not unto thine own understanding. In all the ways acknowledge him, and he shall direct thy paths. Be not wise in thine own eyes. . . "* A wise man is a man who is not wise in his own eyes. He does not look to himself and say, "You have it all figured out. You do not need any help. You do not need any advice. You have life all figured out." That man is heading for serious trouble. Be careful that you never begin to think that you have a handle on everything that God is talking about. Satan will try to deceive you in that manner. Do not fall for his lies.

Proverbs 10:5, *"He that gathereth in summer is a wise son: but he that sleepeth in harvest is a son that causeth shame."* Proverbs 6:6, *"Go to the ant, thou sluggard; consider her ways, and be wise."* If you want to be wise, think about this. "Which having no guide, overseer, or ruler . . ." The ant does not have someone standing over it telling it to get ready for the future. They prepare for future needs on their own. They do not wait until there is no food on the ground and then try to find it. It should not be necessary for someone to stand over you on your job or in your home to make sure you do what you should. *"Which having no guide, overseer, or ruler, Provideth her meat in the summer . . ."* What did Proverbs 10:5 say? A wise son gathers meat in the summer and gathers food in the harvest. Proverbs 6:9, *"How long wilt thou sleep, O sluggard? When wilt thou arise out of thy sleep?"* Remember, in Ephesians 5 we were told to awake those who sleep. But the sluggard answers, "just let me lie here a little bit longer. I will do it tomorrow. I know I need to take care of things. I know I ought to get up and do it. I know I need to get in the Word, but I will do it next week. I just want to sit here a little bit longer."

This remeinds me of Pharaoh. One of the plagues was frogs. You remember, Moses came to Pharaoh one day. There were frogs in the city, frogs in the beds, frogs underfoot, frogs on the table while dinner was being eaten. All day long, everywhere people walked, they stepped on frogs. Big frogs, brown frogs, small frogs, green frogs, dirty frogs, slimy frogs, every kind of frog you can think of. They were everywhere. They could not be avoided. The Bible says the frogs covered the land. Finally Pharaoh called out to Moses and asked him to do something about the frogs. When Moses asked Pharoah when he wanted the frogs gone Pharoah said, *"Tomorrow. Just let me sleep with the frogs one more night."* The next day when Moses told the frogs to leave, they obeyed. But the nation of Egypt had one more night with the frogs. "Charles, I wouldn't do that." I wonder how many believers are tolerating frogs in their lives right now. I wonder how many believers are putting up with problems they are tired of. They lie in bed at night and think, "Why doesn't this thing go away?" God says, *"Why don't you do something about it?"* "I will tomorrow. God, I promise you, tomorrow I'm going to change. I'm going to get up early and get in the Word." Tomorrow the alarm rings, you turn it off and sleep until 8:30. "Just give me one more night with the frogs."

When you begin to apply God's Word in your life, you will begin to see His abundance. Things start changing. You will begin to experience the flow of God's blessings in your life. You will begin to see God's power in your life. When you start experiencing these things, do not quit doing what you are doing just because the pressure has ceased. Keep on gathering in the summer so you can stay in that state of abundance, instead of going from abundance to famine, abundance to famine, abundance to famine.

Proverbs 6:11, *"So shall thy poverty come as one that travelleth, and thy want as an armed man."* Keep putting off what you need to do and poverty will come into your life. Chapter 8 verse 33, *"Hear instruction and be wise. . . . "* Hear instruction and be wise. "Why does my pastor always tell me I need to get in the Word?" Because he wants you to be wise. To be wise you need to make the most of every moment. Solomon said in Proverbs 3 that the wisdom of God is more precious than rubies and diamonds and is more valuable than the merchandising of gold. I wonder what would happen if some evening you heard a knock on your door and a very distinguished looking man was standing there. He looked at you and said, "I'm sorry to bother you, but I have some information I believe you will find very interesting. According to official geological studies, I have determined, beyond a shadow of a doubt, that in your back yard between six and ten feet deep is one of the largest veins of gold in the United States." At that very moment your backyard is as good as ten feet deeper, isn't it? Most people would get dressed, wake up the whole family, give them shovels, and start digging. They would dig until they found it, wouldn't they? Why? Because gold is precious. It can change your life for the better.

God says that His Word is more valuable in your life than the merchandising of gold. That is a strong emphasis God places on His Word. He continues by saying, *"Hear instruction, be wise, and refuse it not. Blessed is the man who heareth me, watching daily at my gates, waiting at the posts of my doors."* What does a wise man do? He hears, he watches, he waits at the door. There is an expectancy in those words.

Proverbs 9:8, *"Reprove not a scorner, lest he hate thee: rebuke a wise man, and he will love thee."* A wise man will receive correction. If he is wrong he will admit it. There are some people who refuse to admit that they do not know everything. The Bible says that before you have Christ in your life you are blind, and walking in darkness. In fact, the Bible says you are darkness. Praise God, when you receive Jesus you receive the wisdom of the ages.

Proverbs 9:10, *"The fear of the Lord is the beginning of wisdom...."* The word fear means "reverential worship" — a wise man worships God. He spends time worshipping God. Besides what you do in church, I want to encourage you to take time during the day to worship Him.

Proverbs 10:8, *"The wise in heart will receive...."* A wise man receives the commandments of God into his life. Verse 14, *"Wise men lay up knowledge..."* What does he mean by laying up knowledge? You do this by studying things which are beyond what you need at the moment. Many people study the Word of God only in the areas they are having problems with at that moment. That is fine, and there is nothing wrong with that. They are on the right track. But they need to lay up additional knowledge before they need it. As a result, those points of need will never arrive. Needs exist when you are lacking in something. But if you already have the knowledge, then you are not lacking.

Let's continue. Verse 19, *"In the multitude of words there wanteth not sin: but he that refraineth his lips is wise."* It is easy to understand how reading and listening and studying will produce wisdom, but how about keeping your mouth quiet? What does that have to do with wisdom? It has everything to do with it. Say, "Father God your Word rules in my life. I will refrain my lips." You may not understand how refraining your lips will make you wise, but do it anyway. When you choose to elevate wisdom above what you think, God will give understanding to your heart. As you make what He says the final authority in your life, you will be promoted. He said the wise man refrains his lips. The next time you are in a situation where you want to run your mouth off, remember, a wise man refrains his lips. Close your mouth and be quiet. Do not feel pressured to put in your two-cents worth. A wise man refrains his lips. Make the Word the final authority. Learn that on your job. Anybody can talk and find fault.

Proverbs 11:30, *"The fruit of the righteous is a tree of life; and he that winneth souls is wise."* It is a wise thing to sin souls to Jesus. It is wisdom for a church to be strong in its desire to get people saved. Proverbs 12:15, *"The way of a fool is right in his own eyes: but he that hearkeneth unto counsel is wise."* A wise man is someone who will listen to advice. Proverbs 13:20, *"He that walketh with wise men shall be wise: but a companion of fools shall be destroyed."* You might need to get a new set of friends. He that walks with wise men shall be wise.

If you want to learn how to be a success in life, do not go down to the coffee shop where all the "do-nothings" go. Do not ask them about success. They are failures. I am not being critical, they can get hold of God's Word and change their lives also. They can get good counsel and be blessed also. My wife and I make ourselves available to wise men. I will not ask a man who was run out of the ministry how to build a successful church, reach cities, or win people to Jesus. He will tell me, "It can't be done. The task is too heavy, the burden is too great, the battle is too much, the enemy is too strong." I listen to people who are doing it and succeeding.

If I were working in the secular world, I would search for a man who had already become successful in the area or field in which I am interested, and would obtain a job with him. I would say, "Mister, I want to be a success in real estate, and I want you to teach me." He may look at me and say, "I don't need more people to help me. I'm not hiring anybody." I would say, "I'm not asking for a job. I want to learn how to be a success." If that man turned me down, I would find another one. Eventually, one of them would look at me and say, "All right, come on. Let's see if you can keep up." If I were willing to stay up at night, studying and learning and burning the midnight oil, renewing my mind and willing to work hard, I would become a success.

When God called my wife and me into the ministry I did not have the slightest idea what to do. I said, "Lord I don't want to be in the ministry unless I can be around people who know what they are doing." I was a spiritual illiterate. From that day to this, we have had the privilege of sitting down and talking to some of the finest ministers in the world. Why? Because I do not want to be a pastor and remain a dummy. If I am going to teach people, I need to be around people who are knowledgeable.

Proverbs 14:1, *"Every wise woman buildeth her house but the foolish plucketh it down with her hands."*

51

There are a lot of people who are tearing their lives down through foolishness. They talk, think, act, and believe in a wrong manner. Verse 16, *"A wise man feareth, and departeth from evil. . . ."* Paul said to abstain from the very appearance of evil. If you get involved in a situation and it starts looking bad, then get away from it. Do not let the devil fool you into thinking that you can go into evil and not be affected by it. You are wrong. You cannot play with the devil.

Proverbs 15:2, *"The tongue of the wise useth knowledge aright: but the mouth of fools poureth out foolishness."* You must watch what you say.

Proverbs 16:14, *"The wrath of a king is as messengers of death: but a wise man will pacify it."* Wisdom pacifies wrath instead of adding fuel to it. Be a peacemaker. What did Jesus say? Blessed are the peacemakers, not the peace destroyers, not the wrath inciters. Be a bridge builder and peacemaker.

Proverbs 16:23, *"The heart of the wise teacheth his mouth, and addeth learning to his lips."* One of the keys to wisdom is listening to your spirit. You need to learn how to listen to the man that is on the inside. Turn your ears inward and begin with small things. Do not wait until you are trying to raise somebody from the dead to decide to listen to your heart. You learn how to listen in small things. The next time you walk into the grocery store and hear a voice inside say, "Go ahead and buy a half gallon of milk while you are here," do it. Believe me, you can save yourself a lot of trips back to the store for milk by obeying the voice of your spirit. In this way, you can learn to listen by acting on fairly insignificant things which are not a matter of life or death.

Proverbs 24:5, *"A wise man is strong., yea, a man of knowledge increaseth strength. For by wise counsel thou shalt make thy war: and in multitude of counsellors there is safety."* Count the cost of what you are going to do to see if you can handle it. "Any enterprise is built on wise planning, becomes strong through common sense and profits wonderfully through keeping abreast of the facts." That is Proverbs 24:3 and 4 in the Living Bible.

Verse 23, *"These things also belong to the wise, it is not good to have respect of persons in judgment."* Do not set one standard for one person and another standard for someone else. That is not how God does it. His standards are the same for everybody. Treat everyone equally.

Chapter IV

THE FRUITS OF WISDOM

Proverbs 2:6, *"For the Lord giveth wisdom..."* Who gives wisdom? The Lord does. You need to ask Him for it. You will need to search Him for it. You will need to seek Him for it. You will need to look to Him for it. You will not get wisdom anywhere but from Him. I am talking about the wisdom of God. He gives it. The Lord gives wisdom. "But Charles, I don't think He will give it to me." Then read James the first chapter. James said, if any man lack wisdom let him ask of God, who gives liberally to all men and up-braideth not. If you ask Him, He will give it to you. He will give you the wisdom. "Do I have to ask?" Yes, you have to ask. "I think if God wants me to have it, then He will give it to me." You think wrongfully. He said, if any man lacks wisdom let him ask — then God will give. "But, Charles, if God knows that I need it, then why doesn't He give it to me?" I don't know. I have not figured that out yet myself, but I do know I am going to do what He said and He said ask — so I will ask. "I don't want to ask." Then sit there and be dumb, but don't blame God. He said, if you would ask, He would give it to you. "But I don't deserve His wisdom. I have too many faults." The Bible says He upbraids not. That means He finds no fault.

Proverbs 2:6, *"For the Lord giveth wisdom: out of his mouth cometh knowledge and understanding."* How does knowledge and understanding come out of His mouth? What comes out of your mouth? Words. When you speak words, I can understand you. If you do not say anything, I cannot understand you. You use words to explain yourself. Through your words I gain knowledge. Through God's Word you gain knowledge and understanding. How do you get knowledge and understanding? Through His Words. Out of His mouth come His Words and in His Words are His knowledge and His understanding.

Verse 6 again, *"For the Lord giveth wisdom: out of his mouth cometh knowledge and understanding. He layeth up sound wisdom for the righteous . . ."* Who are the righteous? We are the righteous. "I would not say I am righteous." Would you say that you are born-again? Are you in Christ? According to II Corinthians 5:21 He made Him to be sin for us who knew no sin so that we might be made the righteousness of God in Christ Jesus. If you are in Christ you have been made the righteousness of God. "I don't feel righteous." Your feelings do not validate the truth of God's Word. We are talking about what the Bible says. If you are going to walk in the wisdom of God, you will need to submit your feelings to the authority of God's Word.

Verse 7, *"He layeth up sound wisdom for the righteous. . . "* He has wisdom laid up for you. Now, I want us to read in the third chapter of Proverbs. Let's start with verse 33, *"The curse of the Lord is in the house of the wicked: but he blesseth the habitation of the just. Surely he scorneth the scorners: but he giveth grace unto the lowly. The wise shall inherit glory: but shame shall be the promotion of fools."* What is glory? The Bible talks about different kinds of glory. It talks about the glory of men. It talks about the glory of God. The Bible says the glory of the Lord filled the temple. The glory of the Lord filling the temple was the visible manifestation of the anointing of the Holy Ghost. Another glory that the Bible talks about is heaven. Heaven is referred to as glory.

Philippians 4:19 says my God shall supply all your needs according to His riches in glory. His riches in glory are his riches in heaven. It is according to that scale that God will meet your needs. He says here that the wise shall inherit glory — which glory is it? Praise God, I believe that it is both of them. I believe that you will inherit the manifestation of the anointing of the Holy Ghost in your life and you will inherit the heavenly city where God lives.

Let us look at some more things which wisdom will produce in your life. Proverbs 4:11, *"I have taught thee in the way of wisdom; I have led thee in right paths. When thou goest, thy steps shall not be straitened; and when thou runnest, thou shalt not stumble."* This is some of the fruit that wisdom will produce in your life. God wants this in your life. When you go, your steps shall not be strained, and you will not be held back. When you go to do something, everything will be ready, and you will be ready to do it. Think about how much time that will save you.

"Charles, I don't run." He is not talking only about physical running. He is talking about the life of faith. The apostle Paul said in I Corinthians 9:24 that all men who run in a race run to obtain the prize. A lot of people think that the Christian life is a hundred-yard dash, but soon they discover it is a twenty-mile run. They take off in a blaze of glory, expecting to obtain everything that God's Word promises, thinking they can save the world in six weeks. When all that does not happen, they get frustrated and tired, and fall by the wayside. Instead, they need to be consistent. Do not be like a jack rabbit runner. You have heard the story of the rabbit and the tortoise. Be consistent. Be consistent in your walk, be consistent in what you are doing with the Word. Be consistent with your confession of faith. Be consistent.

People come to church. They hear me teach on prayer and confession and say, "Praise God, that's for me. I'm going to do it. I'm going to get in the Word for four hours a day from now on. I'm going to get up every morning at four o'clock to confess the Word for three hours, and pray in other tongues for an hour before I go to work. I'm going to do that for the rest of my life." About two weeks later they pass out from exhaustion. Do not set standards so high that you cannot live with them for the rest of your life. Remember, the letter of the law kills, but the spirit brings life. Take what God says and go to Him in prayer saying, "Father, I see what you are saying. I want to bring this into my life. Tell me how to do it where I am right now." He will tell you. Then do it. In a few weeks, God will speak to you, "You have been praying for 30 minutes a day, let's increase your prayer time to 45 minutes.'' Then do it. Above all be obedient. Do what your spirit tells you to do. Listen to Him. Obey your heart, and you will have some real adventures with God. Some of them may be little things, but they will bless you.

Proverbs 5:1, *"My son, attend unto my wisdom, and bow thine ear to my understanding: that thou mayest regard discretion, and that thy lips may keep knowledge.''* The book of Proverbs says that the man who has the wisdom and the knowledge of God on his lips shall stand before kings. Do you know that every Sunday morning and every Tuesday night, I stand before kings. That's right — I stand before kings. My congregation is full of kings. You are a king. Say, "I am a king in the family of God. I am a king, and I reign in my life through Jesus.'' You are a king. As you walk in God's wisdom, you will stand before kings. God may send you to England. Somebody has to tell those people about Jesus. He may send you to your next door neighbor who is a born-again Christian but living a defeated life. You will put God's wisdom into their life, thus changing it. I think the greatest satisfaction in living is helping people. I love to see lives changed.

Proverbs 9:9, *"Give instruction to a wise man, and he will yet be wiser: teach a just man, and he will increase in learning. The fear of the Lord is the beginning of wisdom. . . ''* That is where wisdom begins. The fear of the Lord — I am not talking about the kind of fear which causes you to shake and tremble. That is not what Solomon is talking about. He is talking about the reverential worship of God. That is the beginning of wisdom. That is where wisdom begins. That is the seed, and without it you will never have the wisdom of God. If you, in your heart, have not bowed yourself down before God for who He is and what He is, you will never have the wisdom of God. I am not talking about going before Him and saying, "I'm no good, I'm lousy. I do not know why you even think about me. I would understand if you hit me with lightning right now. I would understand if you just took everything away from me and sent me to hell. I would understand, because I'm no good, I'm so unworthy." That is not worship. That is condemnation. That is false humility. Religious humility. Now, that may go against your grain, but it is the truth. That is false religious humility — "God, I'm so no good" — you don't even believe that! If you actually did, you would not be talking to God. In reality, you are trying to impress God with the lowly opinion you have of yourself. "Look at me Lord, I'm so no good. Aren't you impressed with that?" No, He is not impressed when we talk badly about His child, even when it is yourself.

Verse 10, *"For the fear of the Lord is the beginning of wisdom: and the knowledge of the holy is understanding. For by me (he is talking about wisdom) thy days shall be multiplied, and the years of thy life shall be increased."* "Charles, aren't you afraid of dying young?" No. I don't even think about it. "How long do you think you will live, Charles?" Until I'm full of life and ready to go somewhere else. "You can't live like that." Don't tell the apostle Paul that. Paul said he did not know what to do, he was torn between two things. He said to leave was to be with Christ, but for their sakes he would

60

stay because they needed him. History tells us they cut his head off. They may have taken his body out and cut his head off, but I guarantee you, he was gone. Isn't that a better way to leave?

Proverbs 12:18, *"There is that speaketh like the piercings of a sword: but the tongue of the wise is health."* The Bible says that life and death is in the power of the tongue. (Proverbs 18:21) Say healthy things about your life. If you are going to say anything about your life, say you are well. Your tongue will produce health. Chapter 14:3, *"In the mouth of the foolish is a rod of pride: but the lips of the wise shall preserve them."* The word preserve means "to keep alive and in existence; to make safe from harm or injury." The lips of the wise will keep them safe. "The words that you speak as you begin to say God's Word, which is God's wisdom, will keep you safe."

Proverbs 14:24. This is an interesting verse. *"The crown of the wise* (a crown is given when you have accomplished something — a crown is a symbol of honor and respect — not of failure) *is their riches. . . ."* This verse goes against the grain of a lot of religious doctrines. We have taught for years in our church that the crown of the wise is proverty. Being broke is not a sign that you are wise. The crown of the wise is their riches. Expect to prosper. Solomon asked God for wisdom, and see what else he received. You cannot separate wisdom and prosperity. If you walk in the wisdom of God, you are going to prosper.

Proverbs 19:8, *"He that getteth wisdom loveth his own soul: he that keepeth understanding shall find good."* It is good for your mind; it is good for your

61

emotions; it is good for your will to have the wisdom of God. It is good for you and produces good fruit. It makes things better for you.

Proverbs 21:20, *"There is treasure to be desired and oil in the dwelling of the wise. . ."* He is talking about inside your house, where you dwell, where you live, where you walk in wisdom. In the dwelling of the wise; there is treasure to be desired. There will be things in your life that other people will want. I am not talking about material things only, but about other things — peace, love, joy, etc. Those things that other people desire will be in your house. Now, oil in the Old Testament represents oil and the Holy Spirit. They poured oil on the head of the prophet or the king which represented the Spirit of God coming upon him. This gave him the ability to accomplish what God had called him to do. He said there shall be oil — the Holy Ghost. God's anointing for your life will be in your house, because you walk in the wisdom of God.

Proverbs 3:13, *"Happy is the man who findeth wisdom. . ."* If there is *anything* that society is looking for today, it is the key to happiness. People think they can find it in drugs. Others think they will find it in liquor. Some think they will find it in sex. Everybody is looking for the key to happiness, and here it is. "Happy is the man that fineth wisdom. . ." Are you tired of being sad? Are you tired of walking around depressed? Have you had enough sadness in your life? Then find wisdom. "Where Charles? Where do I go to find it?" In the Word of God! You do not need to beg to find the wisdom of God. All you need to do is read the Bible and ask the Spirit of God to reveal God's wisdom to you. He will do it. I would rather walk through life with a smile on my face, having a good time and being a blessing to people than be oppressed and unhappy.

People have asked me, "Why do more people go to your church?" Because we are having a good time. We are having a good time, loving Jesus. We discovered that He came to give us life and to give it to us more abundantly. God does not believe in blue Mondays.

If any man lack wisdom, let him ask of God who gives liberally. God is not stingy. I have seen people begin to feel quilty when the blessings of God come upon them and overtook them. I have had people tell me, "Charles, my life has become so good, I feel badly about it. My life has become so rich and so full that it does not seem fair." They begin to feel guilty about it. As long as you know who gave it to you, and you give Him all the glory, and all the praise, and all the honor, enjoy it! Even though your aunt and uncle get upset, your neighbor quits talking to you, and Grandma gets angry with you, keep on enjoying God's blessings and let those criticisms roll off your back like water off a duck. Do you understand what I am saying to you? Love them and pray for them. Put your arm around them and hug them even though they do not want you to and think you are a fanatic. When you go to Christmas dinner they all sit on the other side of the table. Nobody wants to sit next to you. Do you understand what I am talking about? Just love them, and keep on enjoying the blessings of God. They will come around, some more quickly than others, but they will come around. Why? Because in your house will be treasures to be desired.

Chapter V

THE WAYS OF FOOLISHNESS

Ephesians 5:14, *"Wherefore he saith, Awake thou that sleepest, and arise from the dead, and Christ shall give thee light. See then that ye walk. . . ."* God does not want you to be darkness. *"See then that ye walk circumspectly. . . "* The word circumspectly means "accuracy which comes from being careful." He says to walk accurately, If you walk carefully, you *will* walk accurately. In your careful walk, God desires that you experience no anxiety or worry. Rather, you are to thoughtfully determine how you will apply God's Word in your life.

". . . not as fools, but as wise, Redeeming the time. . . " The literal Greek text says *"making the best of the time"* because the days are evil. *"Wherefore be ye not unwise, but understanding what the will of the Lord is."* In the previous two chapters we looked at different scriptures which described what a wise man or woman is like. We saw many of the characteristics the Bible uses

to describe a wise person. We also studied some of the things that wisdom will produce in your life — the fruits of wisdom. I want us to study wisdom from a different angle in this chapter. I have discovered that oftentimes we can gain knowledge about a subject by studying its opposite. In this chapter we are going to study foolishness. Why? Because foolishness is the opposite of wisdom. The Word says a lot about foolishness, particularly in the book of Proverbs. I think you are going to see some interesting things about what God calls foolishness.

The first example we will look at is in Matthew 7:21-23. *"Not every one that saith unto me, Lord, Lord, shall enter into the kingdom of heaven; but he that doeth the will of my Father which is in heaven. Many will say to me in that day, Lord, Lord, have we not prophesied in thy name? and in thy name have cast out devils? and in thy name done many wonderful works? And then will I profess unto them, I never knew you: depart from me, ye that work iniquity."* Jesus said that a wise man is a man who hears His words and does them. He said a foolish man hears the Word and does not act upon it.

The literal meaning of the word foolish means *"silly."* I want you to understand that acting foolishly or being a fool, is not something to be taken lightly. Jesus said that a man who calls his brother a fool is in danger of judgment. God does not take these things lightly and neither should we. We must make every effort to remove all traces of foolishness from our lives. When Jesus said that a foolish man is one who hears His Word and does not do it — you had better mark it down. He is not throwing His Words around loosely. He is taking a word that has great power and is using it very carefully to try to get our attention. I want us to read several verses of scripture. In Ephesians 5 we read that we are not to walk as fools, but as wise. So that we can avoid the way of a fool, we need to discover how a fool walks. Amen? Psalm 14:1 says, *"The fool hath said in his heart. There is no God."* The fool has said there is no God. God does not say they are just poor, mislead, uninformed, little darlings. He said they are fools. That is a strong statement. Psalm 53:1 says the same thing. *"The fool hath said in his heart, There is no God."*

Proverbs 1:7, *"The fear (or the reverence or worship) of the Lord is the beginning of knowledge. . . ."* Another translation says it is the principal part of knowledge. *". . . but fools despise wisdom and instruction."* Fools despise it — they make light of it. They make light of opportunities to be instructed. They do not see the importance of it. They despise the opportunity to obtain wisdom and instruction.

Verse 22, *"How long, ye simple ones, will ye love simplicity? and the scorners delight in their scorning, and fools hate knowledge? A fool is a fool because he hates knowledge. If you hate knowledge, you will be wise.*

Here is an interesting scripture, verse 32, *"For the turning away of the simple shall slay them, and the prosperity of fools shall destroy them:"* What is a fool? A fool is someone who hates knowledge, who despises wisdom and understanding. Even though that type of person prospers, his prosperity will destroy him. The Bible talks about the dangers of prosperity. If you are not careful with money and do not handle it right it will handle you, eventually destroying you. It can choke the life out of you. Greed and covetousness will destroy you.

Proverbs 3:35, *"The wise shall inherit glory: but shame shall be the promotion of fools."* Think about that — remember Proverbs chapter four which says if you will exalt wisdom, wisdom will promote you. Here he said that the man who hates knowledge is he who hears the Word of God and does not do it. He will be promoted by shame. Shame is a very poor promoter. If the things which make a person well known in his community is shame, then it is nothing to become excited about. Do you see what he is saying? He said shame will promote fools. That is being very poorly promoted. If I want people to know who I am, or if I want my life to affect other people, then I want to have a better foundation than shame.

Proverbs 10:14, *"Wise men lay up knowledge: but the mouth of the foolish is near destruction."* Keep that thought in mind as we read verse 18. *"He that hideth hatred with lying lips, and he that uttereth a slander, is a fool."* Slander is talking badly about someone. Who wrote this book? Solomon. By the inspiration of whom? God the Father. So God wrote this. Look at what He said — *"He that hideth hatred with lying lips, and he that uttereth a slander, is a fool,"* God said that the man who utters slander, that is, purposely uses his will to speak derogatorily or negatively about someone, is a fool. That is strong. There are many newscasters in America who fit the description in that scripture.

Proverbs 10:23, *"It is as sport to a fool to do mischief: but a man of understanding hath wisdom."* The first time I read this verse I remembered all the things that I used to do — mischievous things. We did them just for fun. We thought we were so cool, and all the time God was looking at us, calling us fools. To a fool, it is sport to do mischief. For some people, mischief is sport. At one time, maybe you did too.

Chapter 11:29, *"He that troubleth his own house shall inherit the wind: and the fool shall be servant to the wise of heart."* The man or the woman who purposely brings trouble to his or her own house, who purposely stirs up strife or purposely does things to bring trouble, will inherit the wind. That is not much of an inheritance. If I walked up to you and said, "When your dad dies all you will inherit is the wind," you would not have much to look forward to. You have no control over the wind. It leaves nothing in its path. All will be gone. The fool shall be servant to the wise of heart. God said in Deuteronomy 28 that if you will do His commandments, blessings will come on you and overtake you. You will be set above only and not beneath. The fool shall serve the wise.

Chapter 12:15, *"The way of a fool is right in his own eyes: but he that hearkeneth unto counsel is wise. A fool's wrath* (anger, temper) *is presently known: but a prudent man covereth shame."* The Bible says that wisdom and prudence dwell together. What does prudence mean? Prudence is an old English word for discretion. The wise man covers shame, which is the exact opposite of what a fool does. A fool finds fault, gets angry about it, and lets everybody know. wise man covers it. John said it like this, *"The love of God covers a multitude of sins."* That is hard to do until you know whom you are in Christ. When you know whom you are in Christ, then you do not have to announce someone else's shortcomings to make you look better.

Verse 23, *"A prudent man concealeth knowledge. . . "* The word concealed means he takes it and hides it in his heart. It is precious to him and he protects it. It does not mean that he keeps it from someone else. He protects it. He conceals it and he hides it — knowledge — in his heart. *". . . but the heart of fools proclaimeth foolishness."* Jesus worded it like this, out of the abundance of a man's heart his mouth shall speak. Whatever is inside you will come out. Have you ever been around someone who did not know what he was talking about, but thought he had all the answers? He was sure he had a handle on life. I know a lot of young people ages 14 through 18 just like that. A fool is going to utter what is inside, which is foolishness. My daddy used to have a saying. Your daddy might have had the same one. He said, "Son, it is better to be thought a fool than to open your mouth and remove all doubt." I used to hear that all the time, particularly at report card time, when I got my conduct grades. Dear Jesus, I do not even like to think about those days.

Chapter 14:16, *"A wise man feareth, and departeth from evil: but the fool rageth, and is confident."* "I tell you, Charles, I have a violent temper. I can't control it. When I get angry I just let it all happen." The fool rages. In the midst of his rage he is confident. Confident of what? Confident that his rage is good and right and will put him over. But God says that is foolishness. Reacting in anger, allowing your temper to rage on, is foolishness. Now, do not think God wants milquetoast Christians. I think people need to have a little fire in them. I believe that,if anyone should have some fire in them, it should

70

be those who have been baptized in fire. Then when we see something wrong we will stand up and let our voice be heard. I believe we need to do that. But on the other hand, you need to watch your life so that you do not allow temper, wrath and anger to control or dominate your life. If you do it will ultimately destroy you. Many people are very proud of their tempers and will tell you, "Watch out, I've got a short temper!" They are confident in their temper. God calls that foolishness. You will come out ahead every time if, when the people around you are losing their head, you keep yours.

Verse 17, *"He that is soon angry dealeth foolishly. . ."* The man who loses his temper quickly deals foolishly. If you cannot control that emotion of anger, then you will come up short. I promise you, in the long run, you will come up short. This was one of the hardest things for me to control in my life. I used to really get upset. I had to learn not how to control it, but how to get rid of it — just as an alcoholic does. An alcoholic does not learn how to control his drinking. He must remove it from himself. He is no longer an alcoholic just because he is drinking half as much as he used to. He is still an alcoholic. I had to do the same thing with anger.

Chapter 14:3, *"In the mouth of the foolish is a rod of pride. . ."* Pride in your mouth is a sign of foolishness. God said it is like a rod. Verse 7, *"Go from the presence of a foolish man, when thou perceiveth not in him the lips of knowledge"* We are instructed to get away from him. Go from the presence of a foolish man when you perceive not in him the lips of knowledge. Do not sit there and listen to his foolishness. Get away from him. "Charles, what if I'm married to him?" Pray for him, but don't leave!

Verse 9, *"Fools make a mock at sin: but among the righteous there is favour."* This verse does not need much explanation. How many times have you known people who were raised in a Christian home and were taught the Bible? They knew the commandments of God but as they grew older and began to enter into sin, they would laugh at it. God says a fool does that. It is a fool who thinks it is funny to get falling-down, passed-out, drunk. God did not say that was neat. He said that was foolishness.

Chapter 15:1, *"A soft answer turneth away wrath: but grievous words stir up anger."* Argue with people and they will get angry. Talk to them softly and you will turn away wrath. Verse 2, *"The tongue of the wise useth knowledge aright: but the mouth of fools poureth out foolishness."* The Hebrew text says they belch it out. Foolishness comes out of them. They cannot control it.

Verse 5, *"A fool despiseth his father's instruction. . . "* We should paint that on the wall of every room of every rebellious child we know, so when he awakens in the morning, that admonition is the first thing he sees. Maybe that would get his attention.

Verse 14, *"The heart of him that hath understanding seeketh knowledge: but the mouth of fools feedeth on foolishness."* Jesus said that whatever you keep putting inside yourself, is what is going to come out. If you feed on foolishness, foolishness will emerge from you.

Chapter 17:7 — now this is a different kind of verse. It is worded a little differently than the ones we have been reading. He says, *"Excellent speech becometh not a* fool. . . " You will not find excellent speech in a fool. What is excellent speech? When you know how to put nouns, verbs, and adjectives in the right place? No, that is not necessarily it. Excellent speech is speaking excellent things. Excellent things are God's things — His Words.

Verse 10, *"A reproof entereth more into a wise man than an hundred stripes into a fool."* The Word will reprove you. It will straighten out your doctrine. He said reproof enters more into a wise man than an hundred stripes into a fool. Fools tend to be hardheaded. "It's my way or it's no way." When you hear someone talking like that, put some distance between you and them. Do yourself a favor, and get away from them.

Verse 21, *"He that begetteth a fool doeth it to his sorrow: and the father of a fool hath no joy."*

Verse 25, *"A foolish son is a grief to his father, and bitterness to her that bare him."*

Verse 28, *"Even a fool, when he holdeth his peace, is counted wise: and he that shutteth his lips is esteemed a man of understanding."* I do not know if my dad learned this from Solomon or Solomon learned it from my dad, but they both knew what they were talking about. A wise man refrains his lips. He knows when to keep quiet. He said even a fool, when he holds his peace, is counted wise, and he that shuts his lips is considered or esteemed to be a man of understanding.

Chapter 18:2, *"A fool hath no delight in understanding, but that his heart may discover itself."* A fool is caught up entirely in himself. His delight is not in gaining new knowledge. He just wants what he already has.

He is content where he is.

Verse 6, *"A fool's lips enter into contention, and his mouth calleth for strokes."* God said that he who always wants to argue and stir up strife to get people fighting among themselves, is a fool. A fool's lips enter into contention and his mouth calls for strokes. Punishment is coming his way.

Verse 7, *"A fool's mouth is his destruction, and his lips are the snare of his soul."* Verse 21 says life and death are in the power of the tongue. The word talebearer means whisperer. We call them gossips. Verse 8, *"The words of a talebearer are as wounds, and they go down into the innermost parts of the belly."* Have you ever listened to someone talk about someone else, gossiping and telling ugly things? When you left, you didn't think it had bothered you, but later, a few hours, the next day, or even a month later, you realized that those things had gone down into you spirit. That has happened to me. That is why I will not listen. I do not want to hear gossip. Do not let anyone treat you as though you are a garbage can. Do not let them put the garbage that is in them into you.

The Bible says in Proverbs 4:23 to guard your heart with all diligence for out of your heart flow the forces of your life. Guard it. Do not let people put garbage in there.

Proverbs 19:3, *"The foolishness of man perverteth his way: and his heart fretteth against the Lord."* What does he mean by "fretteth against the Lord?" That word "fretteth" means "becomes angered, to feel or express worry, annoyance or discontentment." Literally defined it means "to blaze up with anger or jealousy." A foolish man becomes angry with God.

Verse 29, *"Judgments are prepared for scorners, and stripes for the backs of fools."* Foolish people are punished.

Chapter 20:3, *"It is an honour for a man to cease from strife: but every fool will be meddling."* The Bible says that a person who meddles with strife that is not his is like a man who picks up a dog by his ears. If you don't know what a dog will do when you pick it up by its ears, please do not do so. You will be taking a chance on losing a part of the flesh on your hand. The dog will bite you. "Not my little dog at home." You go home and grab him by his ears and see what he does. He does not like it anymore than you would like it. It hurts! He said that fools meddle with strife. If you come upon a situation where people are in strife, leave it alone. Do not put in your two-cents worth, because the only thing those involved will agree upon is that they do not like your meddling. Leave it alone. Let them work it out. Pray for them, but by all means do not say, "This upsets me too, and I'm going to get into this and help." If they want to get into strife let them do so. You pray for them, you love them, you care for them, but leave them alone. The Bible says it is an honor for a man to cease from strife.

Chapter 21:20, *"There is treasure to be desired and oil in the dwelling of the wise; but a foolish man spendeth it up."* A fool does not plan ahead, but lives only for the moment. instead of preparing for the future, he uses all his resources now.

Chapter 23:9, *"Speak not in the ears of a fool: for he will despise the wisdom of thy words."* Jesus said it like this. Do not cast you pearls before the swine because they will trample them under foot and turn and rend you again. Has that ever happened to any of you? Have you ever taken the pearls of great price in your life (confession of the Word, the new birth, being filled with the Holy Ghost, or healing) and cast them out to someone who did not respect them? They trample them underfoot, make fun of them, mock them, and put them down. Then they turn on you and come after you again. The Bible says not to throw your words out to those people, because they will not understand. Pray for them that the light of the Gospel will come to them.

Chapter 26:1, *"As snow in summer, and as rain in harvest, so honour is not seemly for a fool."* If there is anything that a farmer does not want it is rain during harvest. It ruins the crop. He said that as rain in harvest is not good and nobody wants it, so is honor on a fool. Just as nobody wants rain during harvest, nobody wants a fool to receive honor. Verse 3, *"A whip for the horse, a bridle for the ass, and a rod for the fool's back."* That was pretty clear wasn't it? You must be very stern with a fool.

Verse 4, *"Answer not a fool according to his folly, lest thou also be like unto him."* Verse 5, *"Answer a fool according to his folly, lest he be wise in his own conceit."* These verses seem to contradict each other. What are you supposed to do? Both of them are different situations and demand different responses. Sometimes you cannot answer a fool according to his folly, but at other times you can, according to how the Spirit of God leads you.

Verse 6, *"He that sendeth a message by the hand of a fool cutteth off the feet, and drinketh damage. The legs of the lame are not equal: so is a parable in the mouth of fools. As he that bindeth a stone in a sling, so is he that giveth honour to a fool. As a thorn goeth up into the hand of a drunkard, so is a parable in the mouth of fools.''* Why do you put a stone in a sling? So you can throw it. It does not make much sense to take a sling, put a stone in it and wrap it up, so that when you throw it the stone cannot come out. Doing that is the same as giving honor to a fool. It is absolutely useless. You are defeating yourself. Verse 11, *"As a dog returneth to his vomit, so a fool returneth to his folly.''*

Chapter 27:22 — this is an interesting verse, *"Though thou shouldest bray a fool in a mortar among wheat with a pestle, yet will not his foolishness depart from him.''* The Amplified Bible gives a better translation. *"Even though like grain you should pound a fool in a mortar with a pestle, yet will not his foolishness depart from him.''* We have all seen people take wheat and put it in mortar and then take a rock patty and beat it. He said though you take a fool and pound him and pound him until you pound him into flour or into dust, yet his foolishness will not depart from him. He will still be a fool. You cannot beat it out of him. If you take wheat and grind it into flour, it is still wheat. The only way that you can cause flour to no longer be wheat is to change its nature. The only way you can cause a fool to quit being a fool is to change him on the inside through the new birth.

Chapter 28:26, *"He that trusteth in his own heart is a fool: but whoso walketh wisely, he shall be delivered.''* A man who puts all of his confidence in himself, rather than in the Lord, is a fool.

Chapter 29:11, *"A fool uttereth all his mind: but a wise man keepeth it in till afterwards."* "Well I tell you, Charles, I just say whatever comes to my mind. I put my two-cents worth in there." Brother, it is not even worth two-cents in the sight of God. Proverbs 10 says that in the multitude of words there wants not for sin. If you get into a situation where people are running off at the mouth, do yourself a favor, do not join in, be quiet. Be still and you will come out ahead. Verse 20, *"Seest thou a man who is hasty in his words? There is more hope of a fool than of him."* Solomon has said some very harsh things about fools. He ends by saing there is more hope for a fool than for a man who talks without thinking.

James said that a wise man is slow to speak. Do not have your mouth in motion and your head out of gear. When in doubt, be quiet. Say nothing. Just keep quiet — even if you need to put your hand over your mouth. David prayed and asked the Lord to set a guard over his mouth lest he sin against Him. James compared your tongue to the rudder of a ship. Your tongue sets the course of your life. Even though the fierce winds blow, the captain of the ship can turn that ship anywhere he wants because of the rudder. Have you ever thought about that? Though the storms of life blow against you, you can turn your ship, which is your life, in any direction you want by your tongue. This is especially true when you get into a pressure situation where you are almost compelled to say all the bad things you are thinking. Do not do it! Make yourself say good things about your life. Even though everything within you is crying out for sympathy and pity, say good things about your life. Set the course of your ship toward God's blessings instead of further into the storm. Start saying good things. More lives are destroyed by words than anything else.

Ecclesiates 2:14, *"The wise man's eyes are in his head; but the fool walketh in darkness. . ."* Chapter 10:12, *"The words of a wise man's mouth are gracious* (or full of grace); *but the lips of a fool will swallow up himself. The beginning of the words of his mouth is foolishness: and the end of his talk is mischievous madness. A fool also is full of words. . ."*

Chapter VI

WISDOM — THE ROCK OF STABILITY

Isaiah 33:5, *"The Lord is exalted; for he dwelleth on high: he hath filled Zion with judgment and righteousness."* The Lord has filled Zion with judgment and righteousness. Who is Zion? Zion is the church. Hebrews chapter 10 says that we are Mt. Zion. God has filled Zion with judgment and righteousness and that wisdom and knowledge shall be the stability of our times. Wisdom and knowledge shall be the stability of Zion's times.

The times in which we live today are times of great instability. Everywhere you look you find people who do not know where they are going, do not know how they are going to get there, or what they are going to do if they do get there. People are unsure of themselves — there is a lack of stability. It seems that people really do not have a handle on what is going on. They lack solidness; they lack concreteness. They lack stability in their lives.

The same thing can happen to a Christian. Just because you are a child of God does not make you immune from the temptations or the pressures of this world. The same things which make other men's hearts fail for fear can make your heart fail for fear. A Christian can be just as unstable as anyone. Even though you are a child of God, Jesus is the Lord of your life, and you are filled with the Holy Ghost and can quote five or six scriptures, you still can be just as unstable as anyone else.

In fact, the Bible says you can be like a wave at sea, driven and tossed by every wind of doctrine. I do not want to be like a wave in the sea. The apostle James said in James chapter 1 that a man who is like the wave of the sea is a double-minded man. You do not want to be double-minded, because the Word says that a double-minded man should not think he will receive anything from the Lord. There is no place in Christianity for being double-minded. You must be single-minded — You must be stable.

The Lord said through Isaiah that wisdom and knowledge in your life will bring stability. Without God's wisdom in your life, you are unstable. I do not mean you are insane, but rather that you are wishy-washy. Have you ever met a wishy-washy Christian? Sure you have. You may have been one once. I used to be a Christian going somewhere to compromise until I began to understand the wisdom of God and realized that the Word would work in my life. The only reason you become unsure of something or are unstable is because you are not convinced it will work.

Knowing that wisdom and knowledge will be the stability in our times, let's read Matthew 7. In Matthew 7:24, the Lord Jesus said, *"Therefore whosoever heareth these sayings of mine, and doeth them, I will liken him unto a wise man, who built his house upon a rock."* Notice he dod not say whosoever prophet, apostle, teacher, pastor, evangelist, or great Christian musician. He said, "whosoever." Praise God, that means you and me. Are the "whosoever" spoken of in John 3:16 which said, *". . . whosoever believeth in Him shall not perish, but have eternal life?"* Are you that "whosoever?" If you are that "whosoever," then you are the "whosoever" in Matthew chapter 7 also. He said, *". . . whosoever heareth these sayings of mine, and doeth them, I will liken him unto a wise man who built his house upon a rock: And the rain descended, and the floods came, and the winds blew, and beat upon that house; and it fell not: for it was founded upon a rock. And every one that heareth these sayings of mine, and doeth them not, shall be likened unto a foolish man, who built his house upon the sand: And the rain descended, and the floods came, and the winds blew, and beat upon that house; and it fell: and great was the fall of it."*

Jesus is comparing two different kinds of people. One person hears the Word and does something about it when he hears it. He is a doer of what he hears. Jesus said that man is wise because he is building his house upon a rock. But he said that a man who hears the Word of God and does not do it is a foolish man. He said that a foolish man is a man who hears the Word and does nothing with it. He is building his house upon sand; therefore, when the rains come and the winds blow and the floods come, that house will fall.

Think back to what was said in Isaiah 33. He said that in Zion there would be stability, and that stability would be wisdom and knowledge. In the midst of a world in turmoil, the island of stability is to be the church of Jesus Christ. We are to be the place of stability where people can come in out of the flood, out of the waves of the sea, and find stability which comes from wisdom and knowledge.

What do these things — the floods, the rain, the wind, the storms represent? These are all adversities which will come to move you if you are not established or stable in wisdom (hearing the Word and then doing the Word). In fact, these things will destroy your entire life. Jesus said your house will fall. The house represents the individual life of a person.

A man who hears the Word, but does not do it, will eventually have to face a situation which is more than he can overcome. You may say, "Charles, I've known people who have lived their entire lives and have overcome everything. They never were sick, they never had financial problems, their marriage was good, their children turned out all right. They overcame everything. They died, and they overcame everything. I know for a fact that they were not born-again children of God." Then they did not overcome the single greatest hurdle of their life. They did not overcome death. Jesus said, what does it profit a man to gain the whole world and lose his soul? It profits him nothing, does it? When Howard Hughes died a few years ago, if he were not a born-again child of God, what good did it do him? It did him no good at all, even though he had more wealth than most people can conceive of. Do you see what I am talking about? There is more to life than just what you are doing right now. In fact, the things you are doing now on this earth, in your physical body, is a small part of your life. Compared to eternity, the 70, 80, 90, or 120 years you may live is nothing. You are an eternal being and you will spend eternity with your Lord — Jesus or the devil, one or the other. That is very blunt. I could have wrapped it up in a prettier package, but I prefer to tell it as it is.

Jesus said that whosoever heareth these things and does them will be likened to a wise man who built his house upon a rock. Of all of the things you can think of which are stable, rocks would be one of them. The very name, rock, brings to your mind some degree of stability. Of course, the bigger the rock the more stable it is. Jesus said that a man who hears the Word of God is a wise man, because he builds his house upon the rock. When the storms come, to shake you and make you unstable, you will remain stable. Why? Because you are a wise man. What is a wise man? A wise man is a man who hears the Word and does it, puts it into operation, acts upon it, and is a doer of the Word of God. That is a wise man. He builds his house upon the rock. Let us find out something else about that rock.

Matthew 16:13, *"When Jesus came into the coasts of Caesarea Philippi, he asked his disciples, saying, Whom do men say that I the son of man am? And they said, Some say that thou art John the Baptist: some, Elias; and others, Jeremias, or one of the prophets. He saith unto them, But whom say ye that I am? And Simon Peter answered and said, Thou art the Christ, the Son of the living God. And Jesus answered and said unto him, Blessed art thou, Simon Bar-jona: for flesh and blood hath not revealed it unto thee, but my Father which is in heaven.''* What did His heavenly Father reveal to Peter? That Jesus was the Christ, the Son of the living God. *"And I say also unto thee, That thou art Peter, and upon this rock I will build my church; and the gates of hell shall not prevail against it.''* Jesus changed his name from Simon Bar-jona to Peter. In the Greek text, Peter is the word "petros", which literally defined means "a stone that can be easily moved." He said, Peter, you are a rock, but you are a little rock. Because you are a little rock you will be easily moved. This is exactly what happened to him just a few days later at Jesus' trial. A little girl came up to big, strong Peter and said that he knew Jesus. Peter denied ever having known Him. The rock which was easily moved. He said *". . . and upon this rock. . . ''* The word rock there is the Greek word "petra", which literally defined means "a large massive, immovable rock." *". . . I will build my church, and the gates of hell shall not prevail against it.''*

For some reason there are millions of people on the earth today who believe that the rock Jesus built his church upon was Peter. If that is what you want to believe, then you can, but I am telling you, Peter would have made a lousy foundation for the church. That is not what Jesus said at all. As great as Peter was, he was not the rock. God did not build his church upon men. He built His church upon something else. What was the rock? What was the thing Peter knew, that made him like a rock, even though he was a small one? It was the fact that God had revealed something to him. He had received what we like to call, revelation knowledge. He

86

received knowledge that came from a source other than his five physical senses. He could not tell that Jesus was the Christ, the Son of the living God, because of what he saw. Jesus said that Peter knew whom He was because God had revealed it to him. The word revealed means "to make known something previously concealed or kept secret." The revelation Peter received from the heavenly Father was that Jesus was the Christ, the Son of the living God. Then Jesus said, Peter, you are like a rock because you have this knowledge in you. Upon this large, massive, immovable rock called revelation knowledge of my Word — where my heavenly Father reveals things directly to your heart concerning my being the Christ, the Son of the living God — I will build my church. The gates of hell (the literal Greek text says, the powers of death) will not be able to prevail against this church which I'm going to build upon this rock.

You cannot know that Jesus is the Christ, the Son of the living God merely on your own. It must be revealed to you by the Father which is in heaven. When this revelation occurs, it puts something inside you that can be compared only to a rock. It puts stability into your heart. That knowledge comes supernaturally from God through His Word. When you make Jesus the Lord of your life, revelation knowledge does not stop there, but, in fact, will continue throughout the rest of your life. The spirit of God will move across the pages of your Bible, taking the information there and revealing it to you.

Jesus said that when a man hears the Word and does it, he is building his house upon a rock. The word rock is the same word that you find in Matthew 16:18 which says He will build His church upon the rock. You can build your life upon a large, massive, immovable rock which is revelation knowledge of God's Word. What did Isaiah say God was going to set into the church to give it stability in our time? Wisdom and knowledge. Do you want to discover where that wisdom comes from and how to obtain that knowledge so as to have stability in your life? Do you want to have that rock of stability in your life? Then no matter what wind blows, no matter what doom the newspaper writes concerning world events, you can have the assurance that your feet are planted upon the solid rock. This rock is the revelation knowledge that Jesus is the Christ, the Son of the living God. If God be for you, then who can be against you?

Proverbs 8:1, *"Doth not wisdom dry? And understanding put forth her voice? She standeth in the top of high places, by the way in the places of the paths. She crieth at the gates, at the entry of the city, at the coming in at the doors. Unto you, O men, I call; and my voice is to the sons of man."* Who is calling? Wisdom. Wisdom is crying out in the earth today. The Bible is crying out to you; it is speaking. It is speaking to you everyday of your life. You do not need to consult a mystic to find wisdom. Jesus said that a man who hears His Word and does it is a wise man who is building his house upon the rock. *"O ye simple, understand wisdom: and, ye fools, be ye of an understanding heart. Hear* (wisdom is speaking); *for I will speak of excellent things; and the opening of my lips shall be for right things."* Mark it down in your heart and mind that when God says something is right — even though your head does not grasp it, even though it looks wrong — He is right. Your neighbors, friends, relatives, and parents may think you have become abnormal because you are turned on to God. No, you are normal. Peculiar perhaps, but normal.

Verse 7, *"For my mouth* (wisdom is speaking) *shall speak truth; and wickedness is an abomination to my lips. All the words of my mouth are in righteousness; there is nothing froward or perverse in them. They are all plain to him that understandeth, and right to them that find knowledge."* What did God set in the church to bring stability? Wisdom and knowledge. What is the main word that we have used to describe something that is stable? A rock. What are you supposed to build your house upon? The rock of the revelation of God's Word. Wisdom says, "Receive my instruction, and not silver: and knowledge rather than choice gold." He tells us to make God's knowledge the goal of your life, not silver and gold. Make His knowledge and His wisdom the things which you desire.

Verse 11, *"For wisdom is better than rubies; and all the things that may be desired are not to be compared to it."* Nothing can compare with wisdom. Verse 12, *"I wisdom dwell with prudence, and find out knowledge of witty inventions."* Wisdom will give you the knowledge of witty inventions. I believe that. I believe that God is going to drop ideas for witty inventions into the hearts of members of the Body of Christ. This will improve their lives and they will make millions, part of which will be given to spread the Gospel. "Charles, God could never do that for me." You re right. You must believe this for it to work. If you don't, it will not work for you. Look at some of the things which people have invented. Probably every home has a Frisbee. They are great fun and no

89

one ever gets hurt. Why didn't you invent it? You can't tell me that it took a super, brilliant mind to invent it. How about paper clips? Hair pins? Why can't it happen to you?

Verse 13, *"The fear of the Lord is to hate evil. . ."* We read in a previous chapter that the fear of the Lord is the beginning of wisdom. Verse 14-20, *"Counsel is mine, and sound wisdom: I am understanding; I have strength. By me kings reign, and princes decree justice. By me princes rule, and nobles, even all the judges of the earth. I love them that love me; and those that seek me early shall find me. Riches and honour are with me; yea, durable riches and righteousness. My fruit is better than gold, yea, than fine gold; and my revenue than choice silver. I lead in the way of righteousness, in the midst of the paths of judgment."* Why does he lead there? (Verses 21 and 22) *"That I may cause those that love me to inherit substance; and I will fill their treasures. The Lord possessed me in the beginning of his way, before his works of old."* How far back does wisdom go? As far back as you can go. (Verses 23-34) *"I was set up from everlasting, from the beginning or ever the earth was. When there were no depths, I was brought forth; when there were no fountains abounding with water. Before the mountains were settled, before the hills was I brought forth: while as yet he had not made the earth, nor the fields, nor the highest part of the dust of the world. When he prepared the heavens, I was there: when he set a compass upon the face of the depth: When he established the clouds above: when he strengthened the fountains of the deep: When he gave to the sea his decree, that theaters should not pass his commandment:*

90

*when he appointed the foundations of the earth: then I
was by him, as one brought up with him: and I was daily
his delight, rejoicing always before him; Rejoicing in the
habitable part of his earth;* (What was the habitable
part of his earth? The garden of Eden.) *and my delights
were with the sons of men. Now therefore hearken unto
me, O ye children: for blessed are they that keep my ways.
Hear instruction, and be wise, and refuse it not. Blessed
is the man that heareth me, watching daily at my
gates. . . "*

Jesus said that wise man is a man who hears the
Word and does it. James said that a man who is a doer
of the Word of God, not a forgetful hearer, will be blessed
in all that he does. Wisdom says, *"Blessed is the man that
heareth me, watching daily at my gates, waiting at the
posts of my doors. For whoso findeth me findeth life, and
shall obtain favour of the Lord. But he that sinneth
against me wrongeth his own soul: all they that hate me
love death."*

Luke 11:45, *"Then answered one of the lawyers,
and said unto him, Master, thus saying thou reproachest
us also. And he said, Woe unto you also, ye lawyers! for
ye lade men with burdens grievous to be borne, and ye
yourselves touch not the burdens with one of your
fingers. Woe unto you! for ye build the sepulchres of the
prophets, and your fathers killed them. Truly ye bear
witness that ye allow the deeds of your fathers: for they
indeed killed them, and ye build their sepulchres."* Who
is speaking? Jesus is speaking. Watch what he says about
himself in verse 49. *"Therefore also said the wisdom of
God, I will send them prophets and apostles, and some
of them they shall slay and persecute: That the blood of*

all the prophets, which was shed from the foundation of the world, may be required of this generation." Jesus called Himself the wisdom of God.

I Corinthians 1:27, *"But God hath chosen the foolish things of the world to confound the wise; and God hath chosen the weak things of the world to confound the things which are mighty., And base things of the world, and things which are despised, hath God chosen, yea, things which are not, to bring to nought things that are: That no flesh should glory in his presence. But of him are ye in Christ Jesus, who of God is made unto us wisdom, and righteousness, and sanctification, and redemption."*

Jesus is the wisdom of God. He was in the very beginning, before the foundations of the world. He was there when God began creation. He was in the garden with God. He walked with Him. He saw what He did. He was there and found great pleasure in men. He became a man Himself so that He might have continual delight with men. The wisdom of the ages is yours today, because the Bible says that Jesus now lives in you! He is in you! Jesus has been made unto you wisdom. He will be your stability in these times. For upon the rock, that is Jesus the Christ, the anointed one, the wisdom of God, the church is built. Even though the storms of life rage around you and everything looks like destruction, you will have stability, if you have built your life upon that rock, Jesus. He will give your life stability which no man can shake, no circumstance can rattle, nothing can destroy! When those all around you are falling to pieces, the Christ who lives in you will live His life through you. You will see the salvation of God come into your life as you have never seen it before. He was there before time as we know it ever began and He will lead you in the paths of righteousness, into the paths of light.

Maybe you understand now why we are so turned on to Him. He is all there is. He is more to be desired than rubies or gold or silver or diamonds. Nothing can compare to Him. He is the rock of our lives. He gives us stability.

How can you have the wisdom of God? You receive Him. No wonder James said that if any man lacks wisdom let him ask of God and He will give it to you, abundantly and without finding fault. He will come to you. Wisdom is not something, wisdom is someone — The Lord Jesus Christ. How does He get into your life? In the beginning was the Word, the Word was with God and the Word was God. The Word took upon itself flesh and dwelt among us. The Word's name was Jesus Christ of Nazareth. *"Whosoever hears my Word"* — He and His Word are the same. When you hear His Word you are hearing Him. When you hear His Word and do it, then you are letting Him who lives in you, live through you.

Chapter VII

YOU CAN KNOW
THE WILL OF GOD

I Thessalonians 5:16, *"Rejoice evermore. Pray without ceasing. In every thing give thanks: for this is the will of God in Christ Jesus concerning you. Quench not the Spirit. Despise not prophesyings. Prove all things; hold fast that which is good. Abstain from all appearance of evil. And the very God of peace sanctify you wholly. . ."* Notice that is wholly, not holy. Your whole being. *". . . and I pray God your whole spirit and soul and body be preserved blameless unto the coming of our Lord Jesus Christ. Faithful is he that calleth you, who also will do it."* God is going to preserve you blameless unto the coming of our Lord Jesus Christ. You will be made blameless before He comes. Isn't that good news? He is going to preserve you blameless. When you are blameless there is no judgment against you. This is our foundation text for studying guidance. God wants you to know His will for your life. He does not want any of His children living in darkness. These verses lay a good foundation for us to build upon in our understanding of how to know the will of God for and in your life.

We read these verses to discover a very basic point that all of us must know and understand. That point is this — you are three part being. Before we go any further, let me make this statement to you. Decide right now that what I am going to teach you is not hard to understand. It is just different from what you have thought about before. The Holy Ghost will help you make these things a reality in your life as He opens them up to you. That is part of His ministry, to open up the Word of God to us. You are a spirit, You have a soul and you live in a body. We are very familiar in Christianity with the term soul — "Let's go out and save souls." We need to save souls. I know what people are talking about — they are talking about people. But let me say this as a point of illustration. When people get born again, it is not their soul that gets born again. It is not their soul that gets saved. It is their spirit that gets born again. It is your spirit man that gets born again and it's your spirit that the Lord deals with. It is your spirit that His Word comes to.

As you read this book I am not writing to your physical man. I do not care if your body likes anything I say one way or the other. I am dealing with only one person and that is your spirit. I am talking directly to your spirit. I am feeding your spirit. I am feeding him the bread of life. The words that I speak to you, they are spirit. My words are spiritual words and they are going into your spirit. Many of the things I say to you, you may not understand with your head, but you will know in your heart

96

they are right. Your spirit man knows things and can understand and grasp things your mind cannot. Why? Because your mind is limited while your spirit man is not. The food that I am serving you will last forever. It is eternal. The bread of life is eternal life. Jesus said when you drink this water you will never be thirsty again. That is what He told the woman at the well in John the fourth chapter. She said, *"Give me that water, that I may drink of it and not have to come to this well anymore."* She did not want to come to the well because as a prostitute, she was ridiculed by the other women. That is why she came in the heat of the day instead of the morning or the evening when all the other women came. She came in the heat of the day when Jesus was waiting for her. That is just like Jesus. There are a lot of people who think they have life all figured out and then Jesus will be waiting for them right where they least expect Him. She said, *"Give me that water that I do not have to come down here anymore."* He gave it to her. He walked 20 miles to save one prostitute. Religious people would not have done that.

You are a spirit. I am not talking to your body, I am talking to the real you. You are a spirit and you have a soul. Your soul is made up of your mind, your emotions and your will. You live in a body. You can live without your body but your body cannot live without you. Your spirit can live without your body but your body cannot live without your spirit. Paul said that to be absent from the body is to be present with the Lord. In other words there is life outside the body. As a human being you are a special creation. You are made in the image and the likeness of God. There is no other creature that can say that.

God gave you something nobody else has. That part of you is your soul. Animals have souls, but not like the one you possess. Your soul is very valuable. Do you know why? Because your soul is that part of you which stands in the gap between your spirit and your body, holding them together and making it possible for them to communicate together. You ought to be thankful to God that He did not put your spirit in your body without a soul. If He had, there would have been incredible turmoil in your life.

Your spirit man was made for the spirit realm — that is where he lives; that is where he operates. The spirit man is made for the spirit realm like fish are made for water. That is where he was made to run. If you put him in the spirit realm he will take off. You can compare this to the racehorse Secretariat. He was made to run on those racetracks; that horse was made to run. If he was harnessed to a plow, he probably would have pulled it until another horse tried to get by him and then he would have taken off. He was made to run. That is how your spirit man is. Your spirit man is ready for the spiritual realm. Your body was made for the natural realm — for the earth, for the natural realm in which it lives. It does an outstanding job in its realm. Without a soul to stand between your spirit and body, conflicts would arise because your spirit man wants to operate in the spirit realm.

There is a big difference between the spiritual realm and the natural realm. The spiritual realm is infinite. It is unlimited, without beginning or end. Time means nothing in the spirit realm. God is a spirit and the Bible says that to God a day is as a thousand years and a thousand years is as a day. Time means nothing when you are without beginning and there is no end. But in the natural realm, time is everything. The spiritual realm is infinite; the natural realm is finite. In other words, it is limited. The point to all this is that you are an infinite being encased in a finite package. It is the soul that stands between them, letting the spirit man know the desires of the flesh and the flesh know the revelation of the spirit. It is the soul which actually channels the forces of the spirit into the flesh. From your heart comes healing, love, and peace. All of these affect your flesh. These forces are conducted from your heart through your soul. Your spirit man cannot by itself contact your flesh, but it can through your soul.

Go with me to Proverbs 20:27. This verse is a key verse in understanding guidance. People come to me all the time and say, "Charles, how can I know God's will for my life?" Have you ever wondered about that? Have you ever had situations where you did not know what God wanted you to do? Let's be honest about it. There are not scriptures which specifically instruct you concerning every area of your life. There is no scripture in the Bible that says, "Do not move to Los Angeles, move to San Antonio." It is not in the Bible. But you need to know those things sometimes. Proverbs 20:27, *"The spirit of man is the candle* (lamp)*of the Lord . . ."* Another definition of the word candle is the illuminator or the light. And yet another definition of the same word is the mirror. We are going to study each one of these and learn what they mean. They all refer to guidance.

"The spirit of man is the candle (lamp) *of the Lord, searching all the inward parts of the belly."* He is not

talking about your intestines. He is talking about you — your spirit. When the Bible says "belly", unless it specifically in context is talking about your intestines, it is talking about your spirit man. I am going to say something that I am sure you already know. People are very complex. Peter called your spirit the hidden man of the heart. When they operate on somebody they do not say, "Look, there is a spirit." You cannot see him with the natural eye. He is hidden. Science, many years ago, discovered that there was somebody else inside of people. They call him the subconscious. They discovered him and haven't been able to figure out what to do with him.

The spirit of a man is the candle of the Lord. Your spirit man knows everything about your life — every part of your personality. Your spirit man searches these things out. He knows everything about you. Your spirit is the candle of the Lord. God uses your spirit as a candle. If He wants to know something about you, He does not deal with your brain, He looks at your spirit, and your spirit man tells all. The spirit of a man is the candle of the Lord, searching all the inward parts of the belly. It is through your spirit that God is going to reveal His will for your life. Not through your head, not through your flesh, but through your spirit.

If you do not know God's will for a particular area of your life, I think you would agree with me that in that area you are in darkness. You do not know which way to go. When you walk into a dark room you do not know which way to go. You are in darkness. What do you need so you can determine which way to go? You need light. People get caught in darkness all the time and they do not know which way to go. Even born-again, tongue-talking, hand-raising, tape-listening, church-attending Christians sometimes get caught in darkness, not knowing what to do. I have people ask me all the time what they should do about this and what they should do about that. I am not being critical. Please do not take this wrong. I wish I had time to sit down and talk with everyone, giving them all the personal time they need, but I do not have that much time. Some of the situations that people get into are not real easy to get out of. Some of them are complex. Sometimes it is easier for people who are not involved in a situation to see a way out of it. At times you can get so caught up in something that it is hard to see a way out. You cannot see the forest for the trees. Oftentimes it is good to get somebody who is not emotionally involved to look the situation from a different perspective.

I want to share some basic point with you about guidance. If you come to an area in your life and you do not know what to do. NUMBER ONE — DO NOT PANIC. Be cool. Being cool is scriptural. In the book of Proverbs it says have an excellent spirit. If you look up the word excellent in the concordance, it says cool. God tells us to have a cool spirit. In other words, do not panic. You are not the first Christian to be in that position and you will not be the last. God has it all under control.

NUMBER TWO — DO NOT ASK A LOT OF PEOPLE TO PRAY FOR YOU OR TO PRAY WITH YOU. If you ask a lot of people to pray for you or to pray with you, you are going to get a lot of different opinions as to what to do. If you think you were confused before, just wait until they get through with you. I am not saying that you should not get people to pray with you. Find a trusted prayer partner, somebody you can pray with. If you do not have one, pray and ask God to give you one. Develop friendships in your church. Look around. Find someone you can trust and ask them to pray with you.

Occasionally, when I have several different options in a situation, I will get a sheet of paper and draw a line down it. Then I write down the different directions I could go across the top of the page. On one side I will put all the good points and on the other side I will put all the bad points. You will be amazed how quickly God's guidance becomes evident to you. I have done that many times and it worked very well for me. To do that you must pull yourself out of the situation and look at it very unemotionally. You must be honest with yourself, but not nit-picky. You can get so nit-picky about decisions that you never make any decision because you always find things that are wrong.

I remember when my wife and I were praying about moving to our second church building. There were 80 people in our church then. We were all praying and fasting. Then a building came available. It was a tremendous step of faith for us to move into it. It was a step of faith to go from $80.00 a month rent to $1900 a month rent. That was a big jump, especially when we barely had the $80.00, and only had 80 people in our church. The new building would seat 500. I found many reasons why we should not move in. I came back from a meeting and told Rochelle that God had spoken to me and we were not moving. She said that was fine. The next day I was driving to meet the men who had the building to tell them we were not going to take it. I drove by the building one last time to look at it. I stopped in the back alley and said, "Lord, do you want us to move into this building or not?" He said, "What do you want from me?" I was trying to be spiritual. I said, "What Father?" He said, "What do you want? What is it going to take to make you happy?" I said, "I don't know." I really was not expecting Him to be irritated with me, but I could tell by the tone of His voice that He was. He said, "What is it going to take? I have Christian men who are going to lease you this building. They do not even know it, but I'm going to tell them to give you a discount on the rent. You wanted something on the freeway and you cannot get any closer to the freeway than this. It has room to grow. It has parking and besides that there is nothing else available, so take it." So I took it and God blessed us. We saw our church grow from 80 members to 4,000 members in that building.

What I am saying to you is that you can get so nit-picky that nothing is perfect. So if you decide to make a list, make it in such a way that you make it unemotional. Man generally can do that easier than women can. I am not saying that is a greater quality in men than in women, I am merely stating something that tends to be true. Men tend to think very analytically, whereas women tend to think very emotionally. There is nothing wrong with either way of thinking. God made both of us. Sometimes you need to make decisions with your head and sometimes you need to make decisions with your heart. There are times when your head will get in the way of your heart. Your heart will tell you what is right and your head will tell you what is smart. Sometimes what is smart is not right. The world will tell you that cheating on your taxes is smart, but God says it is not right. The best way to live is to have your heart and head in agreement. We will learn how to achieve that in a later chapter.

Chapter VIII

THE CANDLE OF THE LORD

You can know God's will *in* your life. I emphasis the word *in* your life as compared to *for* your life. All of us can know in general and specific terms God's will for our lives. God's will for your life is laid out very clear in your Bible. What is God's will for your life? God's will for your life includes being well, strong, living in peace and financial prosperity, becoming born-again and filled with the Holy Ghost and going to heaven, as a result of having your name written in the Lamb's Book of Life. Sometimes it is not enough to know God's general will for your life. There are times when you get in a situation where you need specific direction. Circumstances develop in our lives which have no specific scripture to tell us what God wants us to do. One of the most frequently asked questions I hear is, "What does God want me to do with my life?" I also hear people say, "Charles, I have been offered a job promotion. Do you think I should take it?" Many people would automatically say, "Sure, if you are going to get promoted than take it. But that is not right every time. Sometimes you need to find out if God wants you to take it. Is the promotion right for your life? Does He want you to be promoted in that area of work? Many times He may say, "No, I want you to stay where you are and take another promotion that is going to come about later on. Many times you cannot find a scripture that specifically tells you what to do. I have had people come to me and say, "Charles, an opportunity has opened up for me in Dallas. Should I move to Dallas?" I cannot find a scripture that says, "Thou shalt not move to Dallas" or "Thou shalt move to Dallas." Those type of things are not in the Bible, but God is interested in those aspects of our lives.

Are those aspects of our lives important enough for us to be concerned with them? Is God concerned about them? Does God want to reveal to you the perfect plan for your life? Yes — to every question. We will come to points in our lives where we must make the right decision, for if we make the wrong decision it will adversely affect our lives. I don't say that to frighten you, but rather to emphasize what I am saying. There are times in your life when you must make the right decisions and sometimes those decisions are not spelled out in black and white on the pages of your Bible. But God does provide ways in His Word to make His Will known to you. "Should I go here? Should I go there? Should I marry this one? Should I marry that one?" Those are things you need to know. He does not say, "Thou shalt marry the first one that comes by," or "The second one that asks." Those are important decisions and God desires to be involved in those decisions in your life.

Let's read Proverbs 20:27, *"The spirit of man* (What part of you is He talking about? Your spirit.) *is the candle of the Lord. . . ."* We discussed in the previous chapter the fact that you are a three-part being. You are a spirit, you have a soul, and you live in a body. Your three parts all have a voice. Your spirit has a voice, your soul has a voice, and your body has a voice. The voice of your spirit is your consciousness.

Before we go any further we need to discuss something. This subject we are studying now is not easy to teach. It is not a hard subject, nor is it hard to understand, but when you say "human" spirit people seem to lock up. Their brains seem to freeze on them. Sometimes when I am teaching along these lines I see people's minds become tense. Do not allow the fear of what is unknown to you hold you back. Listen and you will learn. God will make His will known for your life through your spirit. People have said to me, "Charles, I'm afraid I m going to miss it." Let me tell you something about that. There will be times you will miss it. "Wait a minute, Charles, I thought you were a faith teacher. I thought you always said positive confessions." I am a faith teacher. I believe in positive confessions. But I am telling you, you will miss it occasionally. There will be times when you thought you heard the Lord, but you didn't and you are going to miss it. "Charles, have you ever missed it? What do you do when you missed it? I ask God to forgive me. "Doesn't that frighten you?" No, because God is bigger than my mistakes.

You are three-part being — spirit, soul, and body — and they all have a voice. You have grown up with these voices inside of you. You have lived with them all your life. The voice of your spirit man is your conscience. All of us have heard the voice of our conscience some time in your life. The voice of your soul is your reasoning. And what is the voice of your body? Someone in one of my services once said, "the mouth." What is the voice of your body? Your senses. Your senses talk to you all the time. You hear your senses. You hear your mind. You hear voices on the inside of you. Your senses say, "I like this. I do not like that. I want this. I'm hot. I'm cold. I'm tired. I'm sleepy." Your body talks to you. Your senses talk to you. I am not saying this is wrong. Do not quit listening to your body. There are times when you should listen to it. When you place your hand upon something hot, your body says, "Get it off, it's burning!" If you respond with, I'm not moved by what I feel, that is not faith — that is dumb. There are times when your mind will reason necessarily. For example, when you receive the electric bill, your mind says, "We need to pay this." This is right. If your spirit man says, "We're not going to pay that because we are not moved by what we see," that is not faith. That is known as having your electricity cut off.

Begin listening to your spirit man, but do not stop listening to your body and mind. However, there are things you need to know about life that only your spirit man can know. There is surrounding you, every day of your life, another entire realm of existence you cannot see with your eye. You cannot feel it with your hand, and/or hear it with your physical ears. You cannot reason with it with your soul. It is the realm of the spirit. A realm that is just as real as the physical realm in which you live. It is the realm in which God lives. It is the realm in which the angels of God live. It is the realm in which Satan lives and it is the realm in which all the demonic spirits live. It is reality. The only way you can contact that realm is by your spirit. Your spirit man is in contact with the spiritual realm around you. Therefore he knows things your mind does not know. When he finds those things out, he will convey that information to your mind. Then you can make decisions in accordance with the information your spirit man has gathered from the spiritual realm.

Many people have experienced their spirit man contacting the spiritual realm. They call it intuition, or E.S.P. Outside of Christianity and the things of God's Word, there are people who have developed their spirit. They know things that are happening that other people do not know. People say, "They are just lucky." They are no more lucky than there is a man in the moon. There is no such thing as luck. Take luck out of your vocabulary. Luck does not exist. There is nothing that happens by change. Everything happens by design. Either your design, God's design, or Satan's design, but it all happens by design. Somebody has planned it — and it happens. There are no accidents. That is true in every area of life. Some people think that the spiritual realm in which God lives is kind of a "wooo" type of world. That is not the case. Remember this. The natural realm in which you live today was birthed out of the spiritual realm. The order which you live today was birthed out of the spiritual realm. The order you see around you in the natural realm originated in the spiritual realm. God is a spirit. He made the natural realm.

You can develop the voice of your conscience. People say that women know things, merely because they are women. Many of them know things because they have learned how to listen to the voice of the spirit. They do not hear it all the time, but sometimes they will pick up things. Your spirit will know things that are happening in the spiritual realm. Your spirit man can be in contact with something before you ever see it in the natural. You will know about it before it happens. It is not mysterious when you stop and think about it. You are a three-part being. Even if someone is not aware of that fact, his spirit man is still doing things. He is still listening and picking up things. Sometimes he conveys that information to the mind. You may say, "I just knew you were coming over today. I wonder how I knew that?" Because there was a decision made in the spiritual realm and your spirit became aware of it.

Let's continue reading in Proverbs 20:27, *"The spirit of man is the candle of the Lord searching all the inward parts of the belly. . . "* Your spirit is the candle of the Lord. Start thinking of your spirit, your heart, your inner man, the hidden man of the heart as Peter called him, as a candle. Your spirit is the candle of the Lord. What is a candle made for? A candle was originally made to be a container of light — holder of light. Notice candles do not produce light by themselves. Keep that thought in mind for we will refer to it later.

In Bible days candles were used for one reason; to produce, or to contain, or to hold, or to shed abroad, light. He said that your spirit is the candle of the Lord. I like to think of my spirit, my heart, as being something that belongs to God. Notice God has laid claim to your spirit. He said your spirit is His. Not yours. It is His candle. Your spirit man belongs to God. Now that you have made Jesus the Lord of your life you do not belong to yourself any longer. You belong to Him. The Bible tells us to glorify God in our bodies and in our spirits, which are the Lord's, for we are bought with a price. God bought you and paid for you. You now belong to Him. He has the title deed on you. Everyone of us needs to realize that someday we will stand before God and answer to Him for what we have done with our bodies, our spirits, and our souls. Your body, your spirit, and your soul belong to God. You are a caretaker. He said the spirit of a man, your spirit, is the candle of the Lord. Candles are great, but you can have a whole roomfull of candles and still be sitting in the dark. Just because you have a candle does not mean you have light. You have the potential for light. Now what does a candle do with light? Here is something very interesting about candles. Candles will hold light when it is given to them and placed upon them. Let's say I have a candle and a match in my hand and the lights go out. I have a match and I have a candle. Both of them will give me light, but if I am smart I will take the match, ignite it, and then light the candle. Why? Because the candle has the ability to hold the light that is in the match longer than the match does. The candle will actually bring forth more of the light's ability than the match will. You could say that the candle has the ability to multiply the effectiveness of the light given to us. A candle has the ability to magnify light. With one match and a roomfull of candles I can light up the whole room. "Charles, there is not a match that will last that long." It is not necessary for it to last that long. You can transfer the light from one candle to the next once you have lit the first candle. In fact you can light one candle and keep candles lit for the rest of your life from that one energy source. That one source of light will produce light for generations and generations to come, if it is handled right, and transferred correctly from candle to candle. So candles can and do transfer light. They have the ability to carry that light even further. They actually cause the light to produce more than it can produce in its original state.

The Bible says that your spirit is the candle of the Lord. Your spirit is God's candles. "That's great, Charles, but how do I get my candle lit?" How are you going to get your candle lit? Psalm 18:25, *"With the merciful thou wilt shew thyself merciful; with an upright man thou wilt shew thyself upright. With the pure thou wilt shew thyself pure; and with the froward thou wilt shew thyself froward. For thou wilt save the afflicted people but wilt bring down high looks. For thou wilt light my candle. . . "* God will light your candle.

Have you ever had an area of darkness in your life, where you did not know what God wanted you to do? The Bible says that God will light your candle. It is good to know that you have a candle and that God will light your candle — but how will He light it? Psalm 119:129, *"Thy testimonies are wonderful: therefore doth my soul keep them. The entrance of thy words giveth light. . . "* We have read that your heart, your spirit, is the candle of the Lord and the Lord will light your candle. God lights your candle by sending His Word into your life. His Word is light. His Word brings light, because God's Word is light. The Bible says God is light and God is the Word.

If God is the Word and God is light, then the Word is light. The entrance of His Word will bring or give light, because His Word is light. Therefore, when God's Word comes into your heart, it will give light. It will light your candle.

What is your candle? Your spirit, your heart, your inner man. The part of you which made Jesus the Lord of your life. The part of you that is born-again. Before you were born-again your spirit man was dark. He had no light. When you made Jesus the Lord of your life, the Word came into you and you were born-again by the incorruptible seed (which is the Word of God). The entrance of God's Word brought light. Why did the Word come? The Word came to light your candle. God wants to light your candle because your spirit is his candle.

What does that candle do? It searches all the hidden things of your life. It searches them out. Your spirit man searches out things you do not know, things you do not know in your mind. "What do I do about this situation? What do I do about that problem? I don't know what to do." Your spirit man will find out by God's Word coming into your life. You may be thinking, "Wait a minute, Charles. Are you telling me that if I am in a situation where I do not know what to do, then I need to get into the Word of God (even though I do not have a scripture to tell me specifically what to do)." Yes, that is what I'm telling you to do. "But, Çharles, every time I come to church all my Pastor says is for me to get into the Word, get into the Word. Is that all I'm supposed to do?" Right. You've got it. Get in the Word. Open it up and read it. Go to church and listen to it. Put a tape on and feed off of it. Meditate on it. Confess it. Think about it. Pray it.

113

Sing it. "What good is it going to do?" The entrance of His Word giveth light. "I need for God to tell me if I'm to move to Dallas or Los Angeles. What is it going to do for me to read scripture?" When the sun comes up the light falls on everything underneath it. Everything gets lit whether it likes it or not, whether it was in darkness or not. The entrance of God's Word gives light.

You may need to know if God desires for you to move, and you are reading scriptures and meditating on promises concerning prosperity or healing. You may say, "Charles, what do those scriptures have to do with my moving?" Everything. "Will that help me to know?" Yes, it will help you know because the entrance of His Word gives light. His Word will come into your heart to shed light abroad and uncover the darkness. I know I am simplifying this. There are other things you need to do that we will study later. But this is step number one if you desire to know what God's will is in your life. You must get into His Word.

You must avoid becoming so wrapped up in your problems that you quit getting into the Word. It is the entrance of His Word that gives light. Light is the instrument that drives out the darkness. The more light you have the better you can see. The more Word you have coming into your life, the better you will be able to see. I am trying to remove the fear of guidance by simplifying it. I know what it is like to be apprehensive about this because I was for years. You may say, "Charles, I'm afraid it's going to be me." It must be you — it is your spirit. Your spirit is His candle. In John 16:13, Jesus said, *"Howbeit when he, the Spirit of truth, is come* (Who is He talking about? The spirit of truth, that is the Holy

Spirit.) *He will guide you into all truth. . . ."* What will
the Holy Spirit do when he comes? He will guide you.
Mark this down right now, the Holy Spirit guides. He does
not push. That is an important fact to know when it
comes to guidance. The Holy Ghost guides. Romans 8
says He leads, He does not shove. He does not push. He
does not compel. He does not threaten you. The Holy
Ghost leads — He guides.

For an illustration let us say the Holy Ghost comes
to me and says, "Charles, I want you to come with me
and I want you to do this over here," and I say, "No, I
don't want to do that." He will come back a few days
later and say, "Charles, I want you to come over here. I
want to show you how to do this thing over here." For a
while, He will keep dealing with me, but in time He will
stop. Not because He does not love me or does not care
for me, but I must be willing and obedient.

A lot of people want to experience spiritual things,
but they do not want to be available to experience them.
They want God to use them when it is convenient for
them and on their schedule. However, people seem to get
into trouble when it is not convenient. Sometimes people need to be prayed for at three o'clock in the morning.
People say, "Oh, God use me," but they are not available.
You will hear people praying, "Father, in the name of
Jesus, You said You would give me the desire of my heart.
I'm asking you to use me." But when He tries to use them
they say, "No Lord, it's after five." I am not just talking
about spiritual things. I am talking about being sensi-
tive to God in your home and praying for people — listening to people — being willing to help people. People
have all kinds of problems. They have all kinds of needs

in their lives. Preachers will not be able to meet all those needs. There are too many of them.

When the Spirit of truth has come what will He do? He will lead you and guide you into all the truth. It is the Holy Spirit who makes the things of God known to your spirit. He is the one that reveals to you God's will for your life. He is in you, working through you, and doing God's bidding in your life. He said, *"Howbeit when he, the Spirit of truth, is come, he will guide you into all truth. . . "* He will guide you into how much of the truth? All of it. *". . . for he shall not speak of himself; but whatsoever he shall hear, that shall he speak: and he will shew you things to come."* This is an interesting verse. He says He shall not speak of Himself. The Holy Ghost is not telling you what He thinks is right. He knows what is right. But from the minute He came to the earth on the day of Pentecost, He has not offered His opinion one single time.

Jesus said He does not speak of Himself. *". . . for he shall not speak of himself; but whatsoever he shall hear, that shall he speak. . . "* The Holy Spirit is listening to the voice of the Father or the voice of Jesus. Whatever He hears them say is what He will say. He is sold out to doing the will of God.

". . . but whatsoever he shall hear, that shall he speak., and he will shew you things to come." We want to know about things to come. This is where many people conflict with the Holy Spirit and never receive what He wants them to have. Remember, He will guide you. Guiding is for the future. You need guidance in the future. You do not need guidance to go back where you came from (besides the fact that it's impossible for you

to do that).

Many Christians have a problem in guidance because they have never left the past. They are still living in the past. I know 40 and 45 year old men who are still living in high school. I do not mean in the way they act, although many still act like 18 year olds. I am referring to the fact that they are still living back in their high school days. When they get a few moments on the job they start daydreaming. Do you know what they daydream about? They are not thinking about the future. They are thinking about the past. They think about what it was like when they were sophomores in high school dating Mary Jane. They are still living in the past. Have you ever met anyone like that? They are still living in the past. You will have a difficult time listening to the Holy Spirit, while living in the past, because He is not in the past. The only thing He is interested in is the future.

Proverbs 20:27 says that He searches all the hidden parts of the inward man. He is looking toward things you do not know about. He is searching the things of the future.

That is also where your spirit man is. Think of your spirit man for a moment as if he had feelers reaching out into the spiritual realm (the future), finding out what is out there. When he finds what's out there, he tells you in your inside. Then your spirit man tells your mind and your mind tells your body. Your spirit man is searching. He is looking for things that he does not know yet. That can only be the future.

Jesus said when the Spirit of Truth has come He will show you things to come. Now, if you want to know what is going to come, you must let go of what was. Jesus said it like this, if any man sets his hand to the plow and looks back he is not worthy of the kingdom. I ask you how straight a row is a farmer going to plow if he is always looking back over his shoulder? Do you know what will happen if there is anybody else in the field trying to plow with him? He will bump into them and run across what they are plowing. I know many Christians who are like that. They are always looking over their shoulder. I find people all the time who are messing up with other peoples' lives. They are plowing across their fields because they are not watching where they are going. Plow in your own field and leave mine alone. Let people plow their own fields. If you want to help them, that is fine, but make sure you are plowing your own fields well before you start telling someone else how to plow their field.

John 16:14, *"He shall glorify me. . ."* The Holy Spirit will glorify who? Jesus. What has He come to do? He has come to glorify Jesus. There is a real tendency among some Christians to glorify the Holy Ghost. I heard someone say recently, "The Holy Ghost does not get the respect He deserves in the body of Christ." Wait a minute. Here, the Holy Ghost is not speaking of Himself. He is not down here to get respect. He is here to glorify Jesus — not Himself and not men. If you ever get quiet long enough to listen to the Holy Ghost, He will tell you something about Jesus. That is who He has come to glorify.

I heard a prophesy one time. A woman stood up in a meeting said, "Thus saith the Holy Ghost, this preacher (conducting the meeting) is a great man of God and he is anointed of God and his teaching will change your life." I do not listen to that. The Holy Ghost glorifies one man — Jesus Christ. He is the only one that is getting any glory. *"He shall glorify me: for he shall receive of mine, and shall shew it unto you."* Isn't that great? Jesus sent the Holy Spirit to show us what Jesus has. Aren't you glad? Doesn't that excite you to know that the Holy Ghost is going to show you what Jesus has? He came to show you the things that belong to Jesus. Everything that is His, everything that was given to Jesus, the Holy Spirit will show them to you. What does that mean to you and me? I will show you what it means.

Romans 8:14, *"For as many as are led by the Spirit of God, they are the sons of God."* Notice he said the Spirit of God leads. Would you agree with me that the words "lead" and "guide" have the same meaning? Surely. He said that as many as are led by the Spirit of God, they are the sons of God. I want us to read this verse another way. I want us to read it in a way that I believe will help us to understand it better. "For the sons of God are led by the Spirit of God." The Holy Spirit leads the sons of God.

Verse 15, *"For ye have not received the spirit of bondage again. . ."* Many times when people read verse 14 and 15 they read them as separate statements, as if they had nothing to do with each other. They have everything to do with each other. He is talking about different spirits here. He is talking about the Spirit of God who causes us to be sons of God, and then about the spirit of bondage. But we have not received the spirit of bondage. We have received the Spirit of God who leads us into liberty. *"For ye have not received the spirit of bondage again to fear. . ."* Praise God! God is not bringing us into fear. He is bringing us into glorious liberty.

"...but ye have received the Spirit of adoption, whereby we cry Abba, Father." The closest English word to the Greek word "abba" is "daddy." Even that does not carry the full meaning, but it is as close as we have. Verse 16, *"The Spirit itself. . ."* The word "itself" should be translated "Himself." The Holy Ghost is not an *"it." "The Spirit itself beareth witness with our spirit, that we are the children of God."* The Holy Spirit reveals to you and bears witness with your spirit that you are a child of God. How do you know you are a child of God? Over a period of time, or instantly, the Holy Ghost in your life bears witness to you that you are a child of God. The word witness means "gives indisputable evidence." You know you are a child of God and no one can tell you differently. Your mother cannot talk you out of it. I cannot talk you out of it. The devil cannot talk you out of it. You know that you know, that you know, that you are a child of God. He has born witness in your spirit. He has done that on the inside of you and you know it. Glory be to God. He says that, *"The Spirit itself beareth witness with our spirit, that we are the children of God: and if children. . ."* Are you a child of God? You know that you are because He has born witness with you.

What did Jesus say the Holy Spirit would do? He said He would come show to you the things that belong to Jesus. He said all things that are His He show them unto you. Here in Romans 8 it says that the same Holy Spirit that comes to show you the things that belong to Jesus also bears witness with your spirit that you are a child of God. Why is it important that He came and showed you that you are a child of God? Because it says, *"And if children, then heirs; heirs of God, and joint-heirs with Christ . . . ''* Why is it important that He came to show you everything that belonged to Jesus? Everything that has been given to Jesus has been given to you because you are a child of God, and an heir of God, and a joint-heir of Jesus Christ! Everything He has, you have! He did not say that you are an heir of Jesus. That would mean that you would get what He decided to give you. He said you are a joint-heir with Jesus. Everything that God has given to Him, which the Holy Ghost has come to show you, is now yours. It belongs to you.

"I do not know if I can believe that or understand that for me." You do not have to understand it. Just believe it. You will understand it later. It will make sense to you. I do not claim to understand what all this means, but I believe what is written. Do not let your mind talk yourself out of it. Believe it and enjoy it. Walk in it and you will begin to see God's Word work in your life.

—

Chapter IX

"THE LORD TOLD ME . . ."

Proverbs 20:27, *"The spirit of man is the candle* (or the lamp, or the illuminator) *of the Lord, searching all the inward parts of the belly."* Let me clarify this so you can understand it better. When the Bible talks about the belly, unless it specifies in context that it is referring to the part of your anatomy containing your lunch, it is not talking about that. The Bible is talking about your inner man. Your spirit man. The Jews believed that a man's heart or seat of life was in the area of his stomach, his belly. The Greeks believed that the seat of life was in the head, Paul reveals to us that your spirit man is not located in just one area of your body. You are, so to speak, wall-to-wall spirit man. Therefore, when the Bible refers to your heart, unless in context it is talking about your blood pump or about your belly, it is referring to your spirit. That information will help you to understand the Bible.

For example, look at this verse. *"The spirit of man*

is the candle of the Lord, searching all the inward parts of the belly.'' We know it is not talking about your anatomy. Why would your spirit man want to see what you had for lunch? What does he care? No, the scriptures are not referring to your stomach, but rather to the hidden man of your heart. The Hebrew text calls it the hidden man, or the hidden recesses. I like to say it like this, the little dark corners of your being that you thought nobody knew about. But God knows about them and He still loves you. That is good to know. The spirit of man is the candle, or the lamp, or the illuminator of the Lord. It is your spirit man which God uses to give you direction. That is the part of you God uses to hold or contain light.

A candle holds and contains light. Candles do not produce light on their own. Once the light is given to them, they can hold it and actually maintain it longer than the original source could by itself. If the candle is made correctly it has the ability to magnify or amplify the intensity of the light. The scripture also uses the word lamp. We are somewhat more familiar with the word lamp. Your spirit man is the lamp of the Lord. It is to your spirit that God reveals His will for your life.

I want to clarify a statement in this chapter that you will hear a lot. I make it and a lot of other people make it. You also read it in other books. I have come to realize (because of people asking me questions) that there is some misunderstanding about the often used statement "the Lord told me." I want to explain to you what I mean by that statement. I also know what many others mean when they say that because I have asked them about it. The area of guidance is a very critical area in your life. It is very important and it will become more important as you grow in the Lord. Sometimes there are no scriptures that speak specifically to every situation in your life. I have had people come to me with two choices. They do not know whether to move to Los Angeles or move to New York. They certainly do not want to move to Los Angeles if God has commanded the blessing in New York. Other times people are confronted with choices and you can hear them crying out to the Lord, "Lord what do you want me to do?" Sometimes it does not matter to the Lord. He will bless you whichever way you go or whatever path you take.

Also, sometimes people mistake growth for confusion. You may not be confused, but merely in a state of growth which seems confusing because things are changing. If you will let everything settle down you will discover that, in reality, you were growing. You are "turning the lake over". Things are changing. If you will stay calm, cool, and collected while things settle down everything will be alright. In our church we are in a constant state of growth. As a result things are always changing. We stay on top of it, watch it, and are prepared for it, but there have been times when I went home at night saying, "Lord, there is a spirit of confusion in my life. We just decided to do this and now we have decided to do differently. We need to move one person from a job and put them in a new area and move another one into something else and move that desk and bring another in. This cannot be the Lord. It must be a spirit of confusion." No, it is not. When things are growing they are changing. When you are growing in the Lord you are changing. Sometimes change appears to be confusion because you are experiencing new things in your life.

Many times in your life there will be critical decisions you will need to make. You must have His information. On the other hand, some people will spend hours and days praying about things that do not matter to the Lord one way or the other. I have seen people get in a turmoil for days over whether to buy a white car or a blue car. They will walk around for days saying, "God should I buy a white one or should I buy a blue one? Lord you know which would be best for me." To be honest with you, generally speaking, it does not matter to the Lord if you get a purple one. In an area like that He generally does not care if you drive a white one, a blue one, a yellow one, or a polka dot one. There are certain areas of your life where God will let you decide what to do. I'm not saying that they are not important areas. They are important, but if you are praying and seeking the Lord and not getting any direction in an area I would suggest that you ask Him if it matters to Him. You will probably discover that it does not. What God really cares about is that you are involved in it.

Let me give you this illustration. Many years ago, before we even started our church, Rochelle and I lived in a duplex. We ran our office out of our living room and one of the bedrooms. Eventually we became tired of having the file cabinet in the living room, the typewriter on the kitchen table, and the tape duplicators in the bedroom. We could not afford to rent an office and really didn't need one for just the two of us. To make a long story short, the people living in the other side of the duplex moved out. We rented the other half and moved all our things over there. When we moved in I realized I

needed to buy a desk. Until that time I always used the
kitchen table. So we decided to buy a desk. We began
looking around but I never saw anything I really liked.
One day while in an office supply store I walked up to a
man and asked him if they sold desks. He said, "Sir, do I
have a desk! After you see it you will never want anything else." I looked at him and thought, "He certainly
is sure of himself." I'm not making fun of him. You need
to believe in your product. If you do not then you better get you another job. I went with him into another
room and when I saw it, he was right, I wanted it. It was
beautiful, all shiny, and clean. He could tell I liked it
and said, "Come on over here and sit down behind it. I
was thinking, "Mister, I am going to sit down behind it
whether you offer or not." So I sat down behind it. He
pointed out that all the wood was cut from one piece and
put together so all the grain matched. It was beautiful.
There was no veneer, just solid wood. He said, "This desk
is going to appreciate over the years." He was right. People have offered to buy it from me for more than I paid
for it. I sat there and asked, "How much?" He got out
his calculator and showed me a price. I said, "No, that's
too much." So he got out his calculator and figured again
and I said, "No, that's too much." He did it again. Finally
he got to the bottom price. He said, "Do you want it?"
I said, "Yes, but I need to go pray about it." He said,
"Fine." As I left I said, "I want you to hold it for me." He
said, "I can't hold it very long. I can hold it for three days
only." I said, "Okay, give me three days."

So I went home and for the next three days I paced
the carpet praying. "God, do You want me to buy that
desk? Lord if you do not want me to I won't, but if You

127

want me to I will." I was not trying to con Him. I was really seeking the Lord, but I ended up just wasting time. I walked up and down that floor. Every time I had a chance I was praying, "God, do You want me to buy that desk?" I said, "God, I really would like to have it, but if You do not want me to have it I will not get it. I said, "Lord, if that is not the right desk for me I do not want it. You know if it is the right desk for me." Have you ever prayed anything like that? Three days I prayed and for three days He said nothing. On the morning of the third day the salesman called me and said, "Mr. Nieman, do you want to buy the desk?" I said, "Well, I don't know." He said, "I need to know by noon." I said, "Okay." It was 11:30. Now I was really praying. In my heart I wanted Him to say yes but was almost afraid He would say no. I was thinking, "If He says no, I'm going to disobey Him and then what am I going to do?" At that time in my life $1,000 was a lot of money. I had the money in my account. I could buy it without putting a strain on us, but I was trying to be a good steward over what God had given us. I was being honest with the Lord. Finally the Lord spoke to me and said, "Charles, I do not care if you buy the desk or not." I stopped and said, "You don't care?" He said, "No, I don't care if you buy the desk or not. Son, the only reason I care is if you want it. If you want it then I care. If you want it then I want it for you. I have given you the money. If you like it then get it." I said, "Lord, I don't want to get the wrong desk. Do you like it?" He said, "You ought to see the desks we have up here (in heaven)." I then understood why it didn't matter to Him whether I got the desk or not. From His view point it was not much to look at. So I called the salesman and told him I would buy it. There was not a happier kid on the block the day they delivered that desk to my house.

Now, that is a simple story, but there is a great truth to be learned from it. When the Lord told me it did not matter to Him, that opened up a whole new realm of thinking to me. He also told me, "Charles, you have grown up to the point where I can trust you with some of your own decisions. I have placed wisdom and knowledge and understanding in your heart and now it is time for you to begin to operate in some of it. If there are major or specific things that I need to talk to you about, then I will talk to you about them. But on some of these things you need to make your own decisions. The same thing is true in our own lives with our children. I have a son and a daughter. I make many of my son's decisions for him. I decide what he is going to eat. I decide that he will eat his vegatables. The younger they are the more decisions you make for them. As they get older you quit making so many decisions for them. There comes a point where they start making their own decisions. I am sure most of you reading this book are of the age that your parents do not make your decisions for you any more. You seek counsel and advice, but the decision is ultimately yours. About three or four years after the desk incident, Rochelle and I wanted to buy our own house so we began looking around. We finally found a house that we liked and I began to do the same things again. Finally one day the Lord spoke to me and said, "If you like it, buy it." That seems like a major decision and it was. Believe me, if the Lord had said to me, "Don't buy it," I wouldn't have bought it even if they

129

offered it to us for $1.00. We had grown to the point (and you can grow to the point) where we made some decisions on our own.

I want us to back up to the original statement we started with. It will all tie in and you will understand what I have been talking about. I used the statement, "The Lord said to me." In the above illustrated situations the Lord had spoken to me. I heard His voice. I did not hear His voice through my physical ears. The Lord has never spoken to me in an audible voice I could hear in the natural realm. But in those situations I gave you, He did speak to me. I heard His voice in my heart, in my spirit. "How will I know when the Lord speaks to me?" When the Lord speaks to you, you will know it. Jesus said in John 10, "My sheep know my voice." When He speaks to you, you will know it. I can quarantee it. There is no mistaking His voice. "Charles, what does His voice sound like?" It sounds like His voice. You will know it. He will speak to you some time in your life — possibly in one of the strangest situations or when you least expect it. I have found that many times, not all the times, God will speak to people and begin to build their confidence in hearing His voice when they least expect it because they will not confuse it with something else. That is not a law, it is an observation. It is not a hard and fast law that God only speaks to you when you do not expect Him to. There are times when you are expecting it and He does speak.

But many times when I say and other people say, "The Lord said" to us what we mean by that is this — He did speak to us, but we did not hear His voice. We heard the voice of our own spirit. Our own spirit will learn something by the spirit of God and then reveal that knowledge to our mind, our subconscience, so that we may know it and walk in the light of it. That has probably happened to you on many occassions. We call it many things; intuition, "something just told me," "it dawned on me," "I just suddenly knew that."

Romans the 8th chapter says that the Holy Spirit leads the sons of God and He bears witness with them. The number one way God leads His children today is by, what we will call for purposes of teaching, the inward witness — not to be compared or confused with the inward voice. Sometimes you will hear His voice in your heart, but most of the time it will be the voice of your own spirit. What does that sound like? It sounds like you — when you hear yourself talk. That is how the voice of your spirit man will sound on the inside of you.

Your spirit man is in contact with the spiritual realm. You may have experienced the voice of your spirit before you were ever born-again, before you were ever turned on to the Lord. You would simply know things. It did not come through your senses. You knew them through your spirit. Your spirit man picks up things. It knows things that your mind doesn't know. Why? Because it is in contact with a realm your mind cannot contact. Your spirit can contact the spiritual realm and pick up things your mind can't. That voice will reveal things to you. "I just knew I was supposed to invest in that company. How did you know? I just knew on the inside of me that it was right." I cannot tell you how many times I have read about people who made investments which resulted in millions of dollars because they knew it was right. For every thing that is real there is a counterfeit. You need to be careful of the counterfeit. The counterfeit always pushes, whereas the real thing leads. If you do not remember anything else I teach you about guidance but that, it will keep you out of a lot of trouble. The devil pushes, "You better go, you better do this." There is no pressure in the things of God. I am not saying there are no demands. I should not have to say some of these things, but sometimes you have to. Some people will take a statement such as I just made and think, "Glory to God, when I get my electric bill and it says the bill is due on the 15th that means I do not have to pay it anymore because there is no pressure in the Lord. I will just pay it when I am good and ready." That is wrong.

Let's move on. The Holy Ghost reveals knowledge to you in your spirit. When that knowledge gets into your spirit, then he lets that knowledge be known to your mind. It is the voice of your own spirit. It is your own voice that you hear. The voice of your own spirit. "Charles, I'm afraid it is going to be me." It must be you. Your spirit is the candle of the Lord. You may say, "Charles, how will I know that it was the Lord who revealed it to me?" Because you suddenly have knowledge of something that you did not have before that you did not gain through your own accumulation of facts in the natural realm. I am not saying that studying and acquiring facts is wrong. You need to study and acquire all the facts that you can, but God will supernaturally reveal things to you, to your heart, to your spirit. Then your spirit man will know the proper steps to take and he will let that information be known to your mind. What is that called? The inward witness.

The Holy Ghost bears witness with your spirit. He

testifies of something to your spirit man. Your spirit man in turn takes that new knowledge and reveals it to your mind so you may then walk in that knowledge. Hence the expression, "The Lord told me" — He did tell you — but it was your own voice inside of you letting this information be known. Does that make sense to you? I am trying to remove some of the mystery and misunderstanding from these things. This is the number one way that God leads people. But many people have a problem in this area because the inward is not as spectacular as a vision. However, it is just as supernatural. The inward voice and the inward witness are both just as supernatural as a vision. Do not misunderstand me. I am not making light of visions. I have had visions myself. We will discuss visions in a later chapter. They are one way God gives guidance. But the inward witness and the inward voice are just as supernatural as visions. They are just not as spectacular. A lot of people become confused because they are so busy seeking the spectacular they miss the obvious supernatural that is already inside of them. Why is it so supernatural that God can speak to your spirit and let things be known in your spirit? For God to be able to speak to your spirit and let His will be known to you by the inward witness you must have been born-again and filled with the Holy Ghost. That is supernatural!

Do not pray for visions. If you begin to pray for visions you will get visions. You see, there are four ways you can have visions. God, Satan, your own imagination, and eating pizza before you go to bed. The fourth one is probably the most productive of all. I have heard of some visions that I promise you were pizza visions. The sad thing is they were not as valuable as the pizza they ate to produce it. I want to insert something here about visions, particularly visions which deal in the area of new revelations concerning God's will or God's movement in the earth. All visions are subject to what is written in the Word. The Word is not subject to visions. Visions are subject to what is written. It is important that you learn that.

Listen to me carefully. We have reached a point in the Body of Christ where there is a lot of excitement and a lot of things being said about God doing a new thing. I do not have a problem with new things, but you listen very carefully to what I am telling you. God never stops doing the old things to do the new things. He is the same, yesterday, today, and forever. He is still the same. God does not change. People grow up and He can do more things with them. Please do not misunderstand me. I am not being critical. I am saying that you need to measure everything by what is written. Everything that is taught is always gauged by the Word.

When I was working with Jerry Savelle we went into a church to hold a meeting. It was a great meeting. We were there an entire week. The Spirit of God moved. People received what we said and a lot of great things happened. A great move of God occurred in that church. He did thing in the hearts of the people that we were not even conscious of. When it was over we left town and did other things. We later heard that a man came into that church after we left who had a visitation from an angel. An angel had appeared to him clothed in white surrounded with light. That in itself should have given it away. Paul said Satan himself will appear as an angel of light. This angel told the man that the doctrine being taught in the earth today concerning divine healing is not true. God does not heal anymore and he was annointing the man to go forth and tell the nations that God does not heal anymore. The man believed it. He then taught it to that church and they believed it. The pastor did not believe it, but the people did. The pastor called us. We talked to him and told him to tell the people what the Word said. He said he had done that and it did not do any good. Eventually the church split and was destroyed.

They thought that visions were superior to the written Word. In reality what is written is superior to visions. Why? Because what is written was written before you had the visions. You need to be careful in these areas. God is not against visions. He uses visions. You may have had visions and were unaware of it (thinking you were merely day dreaming).

Chapter X

DREAMS, VISIONS, AND THE SPECTACULAR

It is not hard to know the will of God for your life. All you have to do is read your Bible. God's will for your life in general is very, very clear. It is not hard to find out what it is. But we all get into situations where what God wants for our particular situation is not spelled out in black and white.

I have been using in our course of study the illustration of people being undecided as to whether they should move or not. People have asked me, "Charles, I have been coming to church here and now I have been offered another job opportunity. I don't know if God wants me to move." We all get into similar situations. I want to make a statement about some of these situations. Sometimes people have things arise that really are not as complicated as they appear if they weigh a few major considerations. Let me explain.

Many times people come to me when they have been offered an opportunity to move and say to me, "Charles, I have received an opportunity to take a job in another city and I don't know whether I should move or not. I don't know what I should do." The first question I always ask them is, and I know it surprises them, "Will you have a good church in the town where you can continue to be fed and brought up in the nurture and the admonition of the Lord? Will you continue to receive the quality teaching that you have become accustomed to? If not, then do not move." I have had people say to me, "No Charles, There is not that kind of church there, but we can make it. My family and I can make it on cassette tapes." No, you cannot. That may sound strange coming from someone who has room full of tapes and encourages people to buy them. I believe in cassette tapes. I thank God for cassette tapes. But tapes can never substitute for being in fellowship with the Body of Christ on Sunday or Tuesdays or Wednesdays. If you think you can get along without the Body of Christ you are deceived, and will soon wither. Those are hard words but it is a subject that demands that type of discussion. I have heard brothers and sisters in the ministry who attend a lot of seminars during the month say, "1 don't need to go to church. I don't need to be a part of a church. I'm in seminars all the time." Being in a seminar is not the same as being in church. I go to church and I also teach seminars. I have been on both sides of the fence. You need to be in fellowship with God's people. The Bible says that we are not to forsake the assembling of ourselves together, particularly as the day of the Lord approaches. We need to join ourselves together, be a part of what God is doing, and draw off of the strength of the saints. Even if you don't talk to anybody when you go it does you good just being there.

That is a very general area but let's take it into another area. We are still talking about guidance. These are some things you do not even need to pray about. Many times when I go out of town I have young men and women come to me because they see the success I have enjoyed in my life and in the ministry and they say, "Charles, God has called me into the ministry. What should I do?" Generally before I can answer they tell me what they are going to do. Usually they say this, "I'm going to quit my job and go preach." That sounds very spiritual. That sounds like God. I always ask them "Do you have anywhere at this time to go preach?" Nine times out of ten they say, "No, but I believe God will provide." Oh, that sounds like faith, doesn't it? Listen, I know a young man who believed that way. He quit his job and went into the ministry and do you know what happened to him? He almost starved. I know that is true because that young man was me. I am going to make a profound statement to you. "Don't get off of one horse until you have another horse." Did you get it? That is heavy stuff. "What do you tell those young men or women?" I tell them not to go into the ministry. I tell them to let God put them into the ministry.

What do I mean by that? Start where you are. We have young men and women in our church who are starting where they are. They are teaching children, they are ministering at nursing homes. As they progress God will raise them up. They are starting where they are — they are finding places to preach, but they have not quit their jobs.

A lot of people think that the stronger something is, the more it is God. I have found that the more common sense that it is, the more it is God. Granted, God's common sense does not measure up with man's common sense.

I was thinking the other day about Moses at the Red Sea. Splitting the Red Sea was the most common sense thing to the Lord. It was not a big deal to Him. Look at it from His perspective. They had the desert on one side, the mountains on the other side and Egypt behind them. Why go around when everybody knows that the shortest distance between two points is a straight line? A straight line to God was to go through the Red Sea. When you have the power to split it, why not? It made sense to Him. Split the Red Sea.

Now you may say, "Charles, that's for me!" Yes, but remember that you are not Him. You have His power in your life and you are growing in it, but don't get weird in the name of Jesus. I believe you are getting this. I have seen people make bad mistakes and then say, "The Lord told me to do that." If God told you it will work and it is not working, God did not tell you. I know there are times when you need to stand and fight for what you believe contrary to circumstances. But sometimes people get perplexed for no reason. They should merely stop and look at the handwriting on the wall. In many situations I get a sheet of paper and divide it in half. On one side I list the plusses and on the other side I list the negatives. When finished I see whether there are more positives or more negatives. If there are more negatives than positives, there is a good possibility I will not do it.

Back to the illustration about moving. It astounds me how people will come to church and get their lives straightened out as they become turned on to the Word of God. They see Bible principles work in their lives. Then suddenly they are willing to give up all of that and move off for a few extra dollars a year. You better think about that because those few extra dollars a year can be used up really fast. If you are out of the will of God and not where He has commanded the blessing to be that money you are making can go quickly. I understand that sometimes you are in a job situation where you have a lot of time and years invested. When they tell you you are moving to Mule Shoe, you are moving to Mule Shoe unless you want to quit. You may do just that, but do not quit until you have another horse to ride.

In the last chapter I said that the number one way that God lets His will be known today in the Body of Christ is through the inward witness as talked about in Romans 8:16. It says the Holy Spirit bears witness with our spirit. That witness can be described as a check in your spirit or "the red light came on." We sometimes call it intuition. It is the voice of your own human spirit. It is not the voice of God, it is not the voice of Jesus, it is not the voice of the Holy Ghost. It is the voice of your own human spirit, talking to you, letting you know things by the inner witness. You do not necessarily hear a voice, but you just know that you know that you know. That is the number one way.

Another way that God leads His people is through the inward voice. The voice of your own spirit talking to you. Another way is through the voice of the Holy Spirit in your spirit. We have studied about all of these in previous chapters.

We will now study spectacular forms of guidance. Notice I did not say supernatural. I said spectacular. All forms of guidance, the inward witness, the inner voice, or the voice of the Holy Spirit, are supernatural. You hear a lot today in the Body of Christ about the supernatural move of the Holy Ghost in the earth today. I am all for the supernatural. I believe in the supernatural, but do not forsake the things of God's Word to chase after signs and wonders. God is a God of the supernatural, but not everything God does is spectacular. What do I call spectacular? Visions — dreams — visitations by angels — prophecy. Those are all spectacular forms of guidance. God uses those things to lead and guide His people today, even as He did in the Old Testament. But there are some guidelines we need to establish in these areas.

We hear a lot today about the new wave of the spirit and that the new wave is the supernatural. We need to be careful in this area because there is a connotation being given that God is forsaking the old way and is doing a new thing. God does new things but He does not forsake the old things. This has proceeded so far that I heard a teacher in a meeting I was in say that the teaching of the Word is dead. The new thing is the supernatural. Hold it. Cool it. Hold your horses. Listen to what I am going to tell you. The moment you start seeking the spectacular you are going to get into trouble. The spectacular comes because God wills it and chooses to do it. You cannot make it happen. You cannot make God do anything in a service that He does not want to do. You cannot make spectacular things like visions and dreams happen. It is wrong to pray for visions, it is wrong to pray for dreams, it is wrong for visitations by angels. If you are determined to have a vision, a dream, or a visitation by an angel I can assure you that you will get one. If you are determined to have a word of prophecy someone will eventually prophesy to you. If you are determined to have a vision you will have a vision. If you are determined to see an angel — you will see one. But it will not be God. Remember, Satan is the god of this world, and he manifests himself in those areas. If you are seeking after visions, he will give you a vision. If you are seeking after dreams he will give you a dream. If you want to see an angel, you will see an angel. Paul said that Satan can be transformed into an angel of light to deceive the elect.

God does use visions and dreams and visitations and prophecies. We thank God for them, but they are not the chief methods that God uses. He may use those things and He may not. In addition, just because you have one does not mean that you are more spiritual than another believer who may never have one.

I have had what I would call in my life two visions. They both happened about two weeks after I received the Holy Ghost and I have never had another of what people would call visions. I was on a bed and could not get up. I saw into the spiritual realm with my natural eyes. I have had lots of visions since then of different kinds, but they were not the dramatic type that most people consider a vision. Many people, because of the way they were brought up, have been led to belive that the only way God can lead and guide is through what I call the spectacular. The burning bushes, hand-writing on the wall, angels coming down, choirs singing in the heavens. Thank God for all of those things. We hear alot today that in these last days we are going to see rooms filled with glory clouds and such. Praise the Lord if we do or we don't. Amen? I believe that if God wants to do it, okay, and if He doesn't, okay. We still have the Word. Dreams and visions and people getting knocked down and floating around rooms do not create faith. Faith does not come by seeing angels. Faith does not come by seeing miracles. Wonder and amazement come from seeing miracles. Faith comes from one place and one place only — from hearing the Word of God. Romans 10:17 We are not to seek after the spectacular.

You already live in the supernatural. When you walk with God you are living in the supernatural. "Is this all there is to the supernatural?" Yes. You are right. Don't get weird. God does not need weird children. He delivered you from being weird. God does not bless weirdness. God blesses faith.

It is astounding the things people do in the name of Jesus. "The Lord told me." He no more told them to do that than there is a man in the moon. "He did too!" He did not. He has more sense than that. To be honest with you it gives the Body of Christ a bad name. Settle down. Get real and just live. Put God's Word into your life. Grow in the knowledge of God. Live it in your family, in your life, on the job. Please don't walk around on the job talking in tongues all the time and doing weird things. Amen? "They will know I'm filled with the Holy Ghost and they will want it." No, they will not. They do not want to end up like that. God wants people to be real. Jesus said to take the Gospel and go into the highways and the byways, out where the rubber meets the road. Go where people are. Love them where they are and for what they are. Help them where they are. Live in front of them where they are. Do not try to impress them with how many Bibles you have and how many scriptures you can quote and how many tapes you have in your glove compartment and how loudly you can pray in tongues in your backyard at night. God needs people who are real — not weird.

Let's talk about fleeces. Judges 6:36, *"And Gideon said unto God, If thou wilt save Israel by mine hand, as thou hast said, Behold, I will put a fleece of wool in the floor; and if the dew be on the fleece only, and it be dry upon all the earth beside, then shall I know that thou wilt save Israel by mine hand, as thou hast said. And it was so: for he rose up early on the morrow, and thrust the fleece together, and wringed the dew out of the fleece, a bowl full of water."* Spectacular — but he's not through. Gideon figured if one is good, two is better. *"And Gideon said unto God, Let not thine anger be hot against me, and I will speak but this once: let me prove I pray thee, but this once with the fleece; I will speak but this once: let me prove I pray thee, but this once with the fleece; let it now be dry only upon the fleece, and upon all the ground let there be dew. And God did that night: for it was dry upon the fleece only, and there was dew on all the ground."*

I want you to notice there are five verses of scripture in this account of Gideon's life. I have never counted how many verses there are in the entire Bible, but I am sure there are several thousand of them. It is an amazing thing to me how people in the Body of Christ have taken five verses of scripture and have built a doctrine they base their entire lives upon. The doctrine of putting

145

out fleeces.

"Charles, God did it for Gideon." Fine, but let's read the whole context of Gideon's life. Gideon was raised at a time in Israel when Israel was under rule by a foreign nation. His earthly father did not worship God. Gideon was raised worshipping idols. That was all he knew. He did not have the Bible like you do. He did not have the writings of the apostle Paul to turn to. He was not born-again. He could not go to church. He could not buy tapes or read books. He was not filled with the Holy Spirit. He was a man who knew nothing about God. He did not have the Word of God. One day he was out in the field and an angel appeared to him and said, "You are going to deliver Israel." Gideon turned to God saying he did not know anything about this, so he put out a fleece. That was the only thing he could think of doing.

None of us fit into that category. If you did then I would advise you to put out a fleece. Each of us have at least one Bible, if not three or four. You can go to church, you can be born-again, you can be filled with the Holy Spirit. You can receive counseling. You can read books and listen to tapes. You can pray in the spirit. You have numerous opportunities to know God, find out about God, be taught about God, and to learn from God. Gideon did not. If you insist upon putting out fleeces do not be surprised if you get fleeced. Please do not write me a letter and tell me that you put out a fleece and God blessed it, because I know that some people, in their ignorance, get by with those things. But the norm is that they get led astray. I am not trying to be hard on you. I have been watching people now for ten years and I have seen a lot of them come and a lot of them go. I have seen a lot of good and I have seen a lot of weird. Most of the weird comes in the area of spectacular guidance.

I was in a meeting one time and saw two things happen in a family's life. This is an example of guidance called personal prophecy. This is when somebody comes up to you and says. "I have a word from the Lord for you." I believe in that — I thank God for it — God uses me in that area at times. I would like to be used in that area more, but those things are as God wills. You cannot make them happen. In this meeting someone prophesied to a man and his wife, "Thus saith the Lord, I have called you and your family to be missionaries in Mexico. You are to sell everything you have and move to Mexico and there I will provide." The man and his wife put out a fleece to find out if that was what God wanted them to do. The fleece was that they would sell their trailer house on a certain date by four o clock in the afternoon. Do you know what? They sold it. "Surely, Charles, that was the Lord." I do not think it was. They purposely put the trailer house in the newspaper for 50% of what it was worth. You see there is such a thing as stacking the deck. "Going to help the Lord out a little bit." I was there the night this man received this prophecy. I was there the Sunday he was prayed over and sent to Mexico. I was there when he came back. He came back broke and broken in spirit. His wife looked like she had one foot in the grave and the other one slipping in. They almost lost one of their children who became sick and almost died. They came back asking, "Why did the Lord let this happen to us?" The Lord had nothing to do with it. God had no more called that family to be a missionary family than elephants live in trees.

Personal prophecies are great and God can use them, but we do not have a lot of that going on in our church that I know about. I do not have little bless me clubs where this one prophesies to that one. I have seen the destruction it causes. If someone should give you a personal prophecy about something God has not already witnessed in your heart, take it, put it up on the shelf, and keep right on doing what you are doing. If it was the Lord it will come to pass. If it was not the Lord you do not want to mess with it anyway. God is perfect, but His instruments some times miss the signal. I have people prophesy things to me. Some of them were right down the line from God. Some of them were far out. I do not want you to get in trouble. I want you to be steady, solid, and established in the Word of God so that in five years you are just as solid as you are now and still walking with God.

Isn't that what you want? Don't get off base. I do not want to get off base. I want to stay up right next to Him as close as I can be. I want to dwell in the secret place of the most High and abide under the shadow of the Almighty. You need to take personal prophecies and weigh them with what you know God has already said to you in your life. If it does not match, put it on the shelf. I have had people say things to me, tremendous things, but I already knew them in my life. The things I did not know I took and put on the shelf. Some of the things poeple have said to me I did not even need to put on the shelf. I just threw them out. I have seen people do strange things because somebody told them to do it. It is a lot easier for God to get across to you His will for your life, than it is for Him to get across to me His will for your life.

148

I can assure you of that. You are much more interested in your life than I am. I am not saying that to be mean and you should not take it to be mean. It is merely a statement of fact.

It is not difficult to sound and act spiritually. In any service, if I wanted to, after picking out a couple of people I could talk powerfully and look very anointed and say thees and thous and yea. I could have some of them people packed up and leaving for Mexico that night. I am not kidding you. When you teach as much as I do you learn a few things about people. It is not hard to get people worked up. If it hurts your image of me because I told you that, I am sorry. I am not trying to play games with you. I want you to know the truth. We do not want you to go to the right or to the left. I want you to stay right in the middle. Jesus said the way to life is narrow, but broad is the path that leads to destruction. I have found that the path which leads to destruction is on either side of the path that leads to life.

God uses dreams, visions, prophecies, and visitations of angels. If they come, praise the Lord, if they do not, praise the Lord. Amen? Jesus said blessed are they that have not seen and believe. You are not more spiritual because you have a vision, and you are not less spiritual because you do not have a vision. "How come I never get a vision?" Maybe you do not need one. God is not Hollywood. It is not His job to put out movies for you to watch to keep you entertained and inspired. He has given you His Word. That Word is the foundation upon which you build your life. Not a dream, not a vision, not a prophecy, not a visitation. Jesus said any man that hears His Word and does it is like a wise man who built his house upon the rock. Being a doer of the Word is the foundation upon which you build your life. That is what you need to seek after. Jesus said to seek first His kingdom and His righteousness and all these things will be added to you. Do not seek after visions and dreams. If they do not come, do not worry about it. Remember, all dreams, visions, prophecies, and visitations by angels are subject to the written Word of God. The Word is not subject to your visions — visions are subject to the Word. God does not deny Himself.

Oftentimes people will miss the inward witness because they are so busy seeking after spectacular things. You need to seek God. If the spectacular comes, receive it. If it doesn't, you go on seeking God.

If I had waited for a word from God to start my church I would still be waiting. If I had waited for a prophecy I would still be waiting. T. L. Osborn who has preached around the world in over 70 countries and won an estimated 10 million people to the Lord Jesus, says he is still waiting to be called to preach. As a ten year old boy his parents give him a small printing press for Christmas. He cut up grocery sacks, and set the type, and printed John 3:16 on the paper. He went through his small farming town and put his homemade tracts in the doors of houses. T. L. Osborn says he is still waiting to be called. Surely God called him and he obeyed God's Word, but he did not have a vision or a dream. He simply did what he knew in his heart God wanted him to do. That is the best way.

You can get that inward witness anywhere, any time, any place, but you might not get a dream. You might not get a vision. You might not have an angel come down and tell you something. When in doubt, do what is right. Years ago Rochelle and I made a decision that when we were not exactly sure what to do we would choose the hardest thing to do and go that way. We would much rather have God tell us not to go that way and back off then choose the simplest and have to start over. Remember I Thessalonians 5:21 says to prove all things. Prove them. Test them. Do not just jump out because something happens. Prove it.

The Bible talks about three kinds of visions that occur in the scriptures. We will give them names for illustration purposes. The first one is called a trance. When Peter was up on the housetop in Acts the 10th chapter the Bible says he fell into a trance. When he fell into the trance his senses were suspended and all he was aware of was what he could see. God supernaturally took over his being. He could not move. He could not have left if he had wanted to.

Cornelius, who had been in prayer, saw an angel. The angel told him to go and seek out a man called Peter. He would come and tell him the good news he was seeking after. Cornelius did not fall into a trance. He had what is called for study purposes, a spiritual vision. He saw something, but he saw it in the spiritual realm. An angel did not appear to him in the natural realm. He saw it in the spiritual realm. That is the most common type of vision. Many people have that type of vision and do not know it. God will show them something in the spiritual realm — something that is going to happen. Many times when I am in prayer for a service God will show me things. He will show me people and me doing things with them in the service. Sometimes I will be shaving and

God will show me something in my mind. I do not fall into a trance. While in the trance, Peter saw a sheet come down from heaven. The sheet unfolded to show all kinds of different animals. Some were clean and some unclean. A voice said for Peter to rise, kill, and eat. Notice what Peter did. Peter proved it with the written Word of God that he knew at the time and said, "Not so Lord, for I have never eaten anything unclean." People have read that and said, "That was not very smart of Peter." Peter was not being dumb. God did not chasten him for his reply. Peter was proving that vision by the Word of God that he knew at that time. He did not have the writings of Paul. Paul was still persecuting the church. All he had was the Old Testament and the things that Jesus had said. That is all he had going for him. Three times he had the same vision and every time Peter responded the same. The last time it appeared the Lord spoke to him and said, "Do not declare those things unclean that I have declared to be clean for I have sent you to be a light unto the Gentiles." Then Peter remembered that Jesus had said that the Spirit would be poured out upon all flesh, and that the Gentiles would see a great light and that light was the Gospel. Then the Spirit told him that three men were at his door and he was to go with them for they were going to take him to Cornelius so the Word would come unto the Gentiles. Notice, even when Peter had a spectacular vision he proved it by the Word of God — and notice God was not upset at him. He wants you to check things out. Faith in God is not blind faith. It is seeing faith.

Then there is what is called an open vision. That is what Paul had on the road to Damascus. He had an open vision. He was not in a trance; His eyes were open and his senses were still intact. He saw something. God opened his eyes like He did for the prophet's servant so he could see the mountains rimmed with chariots of fire. He also had an open vision. God let him see into the supernatural realm.

God does use the spectacular. We thank God when it comes, but we do not seek after it. If God wants to give you a vision or a dream fine, but if He doesn't just go on with your life. You do not have any scriptural grounds to pray for dreams, visions, and visitations. If you insist upon doing so you will end up in trouble.

Chapter XI

RENEWING YOUR MIND AND ENERGIZING YOUR SPIRIT

In the last chapter we talked about the spectacular forms of guidance — dreams, visions, visitations of angels, and words of prophesy. I told you that you need to be very careful with those things. Do not seek after them, do not look after them, do not pray for them, do not ask God to give you a vision or a dream or a prophesy or anything of that nature. If God decides to do so that is fine, if not, then you have the other methods that God uses to make His will known in your life. We do not have a lot of prophecying in our church and it is not because I'm against it. I am not against gifts of the spirit. I believe in the gifts of the spirit. When God has spoken to us through the gift or prophecy or tongues or interpretation of tongues it has always been good and it has ministered to us. Sometimes we may go months without the Lord ever ministering to us in that way and that is alright. We don't work any thing up. We let Him do it. I have heard people give prophecies — "yea, yea, nay, nay, you're so special to me, I love you, don't you know how much I love you." Once you have heard that you have heard it and it is time to move on, but sometimes people get into things and a lot of times it is not the Lord — it is that person.

A pastor that I know related an incident that I want to share with you. One time in a church service a man began to prophesy. He said, "Don't be afraid my little children because you know that I will never leave you nor forsake you. I will be with you to the ends of the earth. Yes, thus saith the Lord, yes, I will be with you even as I was with Noah as he led the nation of Israel out of Egypt." After he sat down he realized what he had said and jumped back up and said, "Thus saith the Lord. The Lord hath made a mistake. I will be with you even as Moses was with the nation of Israel." On another occasion a man began to prophesy and said, "Oh, my little children don't be afraid, don't be dismayed. I understand what it is like to be afraid for thus saith the Lord, sometimes I get a little afraid myself." What I am telling you is that there is the real thing and then there is the other thing. Remember any prophesy that is ever given is judged by the Word of God. Just because someone surrounds something they say with "thus saith the Lord" does not make it the Lord.

Romans 12:1, *"I beseech you therefore, brethren, by the mercies of God, that ye present your bodies a living sacrifice, holy, acceptable unto God, which is your reasonable service. And be not conformed to this world: but be ye transformed by the renewing of your mind, that ye*

*may prove what is that good, and acceptable, and per-
fect, will of God.*

In this chapter I want to share with you two things.
Number one — I want to share with you about renewing your mind. Number two — about how to energize
your own human spirit for creative results to where you
can have God's power flowing in your heart. Actually
they work hand in hand and that is why I put them
together in this chapter. While you are doing one you are
doing the other.

Romans 12:2, *"And be not conformed to this world:
but be ye transformed by the renewing of your mind,
that ye may prove what is that good, and acceptable,
and perfect, will of God."* Notice that Paul, by the direction of the Holy Spirit, tied together the renewing of your
mind with your ability to know the will of God in your
life. I have heard people say that there are three wills of
God — the good, the acceptable and the perfect will of
God. I do not think God has a plan A, plan B and plan C.
I think He has one plan and you either obey it or you
don't. Some people would argue with that and say,
*"Charles, God called you and Rochelle into the minis-
try and He called you to pastor the Abundant Living
Faith Center in El Paso. That was His perfect will. If you
were a pastor somewhere else that would have been His
acceptable will."* I do not agree with that. I think God
had one will for our life, and that will is to be in the ministry and pastor the Abundant Living Faith Center in El
Paso and anything we would have done other than that
would have been our own decision. It would not have
been God's acceptable will or His good will, for it would
not have been God's will at all. I believe God has one

157

will and we must find that will and obey it. Of course His perfect will is His good will and it is His acceptable will.

He tells us that through the renewing of our minds three things take place. Number one — we are not conformed to the world. Number two — we are transformed. Number three — we discover the will of God. In the believer's life having your mind renewed is very important. Because it is so important it demands our time, study and effort. The word renewed literally means, "to restore to an original state of freshness, vigor, life, or beauty."

Have you ever watched someone refinish furniture? What are they doing to it? They are restoring it back to it's original condition. They strip away the things that were put on the wood to bring out the original beauty. We are to renew our minds or restore them back to their original condition. What is the original condition God is talking about? Does He want your mind the way it was when you were born, totally ignorant of everything? No. What is the original condition that God wants? He wants our minds to be like Adam's mind was in the garden before the fall — sharp, clear, productive, efficient, nonpolluted. Now from the day you were born your mind has been receiving information — some good and some bad.

The more that science studies the human mind the less science knows about it. It is a magnificent creation. It is a fabulous organ that God has placed in your being. I want you to think of your mind as a computer. We live in a computer age. Everyone has computers or is planning on getting one. Computers were originally designed after the human mind. Your mind has within itself the ability to store unlimited amounts of information. As far as science knows they can not measure how much information the human mind can store. It is practically unlimited in it's ability to receive and store information. One thing that makes the human mind so unlimited is that it checks itself. When you receive new information your mind will cast out the old information, but sometimes not without a real battle. I remember when I was in school and they began teaching us the new math. My mind would struggle learning that. I wanted to go back to two apples plus two apples equals four apples. But eventually I learned enough to get out of school. I had no desire to become an expert in that area.

Your mind can grasp information and store it and use it at a later date. That can work for you and it can work against you. When you made Jesus the Lord of your life, you became a child of God through the process which is called the new birth. Your spirit man is what changed. Practically nothing happened to your mind. You can get born again and gloriously filled with the Holy Spirit and pray in tongues for hours and when you get up the next morning you will still think the same way you thought the day before. You will still have the same thought patterns, the same reasoning patterns, the same beliefs in your mind. This can present a conflict in your life and God addresses that area in Romans 12 and Romans 8.

He said for us to renew our minds. When you become a born-again child of God you need to go on a search — a search across the storage facilities of your mind and get everything out that is contrary to God's

Word. Needless to say you are not going to do that in a month. It took more than a month to get it all in you. Remember not everything that is in your mind is bad. There are a lot of things that you have learned over the years that are good. In fact, much of information you have learned is good information. There are areas though that you can get into conflict. You learn things over the years — remember your mind is like a computer — it stores what you learn. The mind not only has the ability to store information, it also has the ability to to reason. It can take the information that you give it, store it and then build foundations upon that information based on it's own reasonings. The mind has the ability to reason. That is a good ability to have but it can also present you with a conflict when you begin to renew it. If the mind has something that it has reasoned out, built upon, and achieved a measure of success with over the years, when you begin to replace it with new information it may try to fight you.

Let me give you an illustration to help you understand this better. I am not using this illustration to be critical in anyway, I am using it because it is so obvious. Over a period of years as we were growing up if we became sick our minds received information and it reasoned out a formula to get well. That is how our minds worked. You became sick. Your mind went into action like a computer and it popped out the card on sickness. It read, sickness — go to the doctor — get a shot equals feeling better. Again, I am not being critical of that. I am making an illustration. Now you may have lived with that for 10 years, 15 years, maybe even 40 years. That is all you ever knew. That is all the information you had about sickness.

Suddenly you start going to church, and find out that the Bible says Jesus bore your sicknesses and carried your pains and by His stripes you were healed. You learn the Bible principle of the confession of faith and speaking to the mountain. You learn the Bible principle of standing upon the Word of God and Proverbs 4:20-22 about taking God's Word as medicine to your flesh. You learn all that. You have never tested it, you just learned it. In reality, all it is at that point is spiritual knowledge.

Then you get up one morning and you don't feel so good and your mind immediately pops out the card on sickness and reads it across your mind but your spirit man say, "No, we are not going to do that. Jesus bore our sicknesses and carried our pains and by His stripes we were healed. I'm going to pray and stand on the Word of God and receive my healing supernaturally." At that point your mind may give you a battle. Why? Not because it does not want to believe the Word, but because it has not had the time to reason the truthfulness of those statements and the reality of them working in your life before. It has never been able to reason it out and see it produce in your body. It knows that the shot is painful but that it has produced in the past a measure of success. Your mind will be the first one to tell you that it did not work every time, but sometimes it is better than nothing. Your mind may speak to you and say, "Now wait a minute. What do you mean by His stripes we were healed? Your mind will do it's best to protect you from foolishness, and your mind will question you and say, "What do you mean we're not going to go to the doctor? We may die." You need to take the time to renew your mind and put new information on the computer card in your mind.

161

I want to say at this point that there is nothing wrong with going to the doctor or taking medicine. I was merely making an illustration. If you set out and do the things that I am going to share with you eventually you will renew your mind. I am not saying that the illustration I gave you was bad information. There is a better way but we all walk where we are at. If you are in a situation in your life and you need to go to the doctor, then go, but pray before you go. Don't let anyone poke around on your body until you have prayed about it first. I am not being critical. I thank God for everything medicine is doing to end suffering, but even then people get in situations where there is nothing that the world's system can do for them.

God desires for each of us to know His perfect will in our lives and that will can only be known by the renewed mind. Why is that? "Why can't I just get strong in my spirit Charles, and leave my mind alone?" Because your mind is what tells your body what to do and if your mind is not in tune with the Word of God, and the will of God, and with your spirit it will have a very difficult time getting in contact with the voice of your own human spirit. You must get your mind renewed. You must think a new way

Romans 8:5, *"For they that are after the flesh do mind the things of the flesh; but they that are after the*

162

Spirit the things of the Spirit. For to be carnally minded is death; but to be spiritually minded is life and peace." Would you rather have peace than death? *"Because the carnal mind is enmity (or at war) against God: for it is not subject to the law of God, neither indeed can be. So then they that are in the flesh cannot please God."* In these verses he talks about the carnal mind and the spiritual mind. Before you got turned on to the Lord and to the Word of God and the things of God, the vast majority of information you received into your mind came through your five senses. We will call that, for purposes of illustration, sense knowledge. Sense knowledge is knowledge you gained through your senses. Maybe it was knowledge that other people gained through their senses and then they put it in a book and you read it. Not all sense knowledge is bad knowledge. Some of it is good. You need it. The knowledge you have gained about driving a car you gained through sense knowledge. Please don't go out and start driving your car spiritually, drive your car through sense knowledge. I saw a man in El Paso on the freeway driving with his eyes closed, hands raised up, praying in tongues. That is not faith. That is a rolling disaster.

All the knowledge that you gain through the senses is not bad but some of it is. Many of us were taught and led to believe that God does not heal anymore and we have had to renew our minds. Some of us were taught and led to believe that God does not care about finances and if you wanted to be a Christian you had to be poor. We had to renew our mind. You have had to renew your mind to the confession of faith. You have had to renew your mind to the baptism of the Holy Spirit and speaking in other tongues. You have had to renew your mind to a lot of things. The number one thing that works in the carnal mind is religion. Religion works in the mind. It has nothing to do with your spirit.

You learn to trust in the information that you are given and you can always tell whether people have the Word of God in their hearts when they get in trouble. When they get in trouble, they will always turn to the thing they trust in. You will become what you spend your time looking at and listening to. You are a product today of what you have looked at and listened to. You are a product of your environment and of the things you have seen and heard. All of us have had times in our lives since we became Christians that were real battles internally. You wanted to believe a promise but your mind fought you. It really gave you a conflict, and it seemed like fear would just well up on the inside of you and short-circuit your faith. You overcome these things by the renewing of your mind.

When I got turned on to the Word of God I began a diligent search of my mind and I began to look at and pull out what I call the skeltons in the closet. Pull out every area of your life and look at it in the light of God's Word and make sure that what is in your mind is what God has said. If you want to prove the will of God in your life you must renew your mind. Do not come up to me after service and ask me to lay hands on you and pray for you that God will renew your mind. There is no scriptural basis for that. As Brother Hagin has said, the people that practice that are laying empty hands on empty heads. People always want a quick scheme, a short-cut. A get rich, get healed, get renewed, get prosperous, get strong quick scheme. *"Lose 95 pounds in three days on this diet."* You know when you buy it that it is physically impossible. Do you know that in America alone there are over 6,000 different kinds of diets on the market? Some people have tried every one of them. And you know as well as I do that none of them will ever work until the person decides that they are going to do it for the rest of their life. I know people that have lost mountains of weight. I mean hundreds, and hundreds, and hundreds of pounds. As soon as they quit dieting they gain it back.

I could also talk about people quitting smoking. There are people that throw away more packs of cigarettes than they smoke, but they always keep smoking and they know it will kill them. It's hard for me to understand how they can keep on smoking. You know as well as I do they will never quit until they decide to quit for the rest of their life. In other words, you can not keep looking back over your shoulder. You are going to quit and leave it there and go on. You are not going to keep looking back because you will reach back. I know men that get convicted about quitting smoking and roll down the window and throw them out, and drive around the block and come back and pick them up.

Let's take it over into another area — gossiping. There are people that know good and well that God is against gossip. They know God puts murderers and gossipers in the same verse of scripture in Galatians the fifth chapter. They say, "I need to quit" because I have said something about it or Rochelle said something about it and they get convicted about it and go home, and they do so good while they are asleep. But first thing in the morning, "I know I shouldn't be telling you this but. . . ."

165

If that is what you have to say then don't say it. If you know you shouldn't then don't. You know you will not quit until you make a decision that you are not going to do it ever again for the rest of your life. You are not just going to abstain from it for Lent. You are going to do it for the rest of your life. That is the key to overcoming things, along with God's power working in your life. But that is the key. You must make your own decision and you must make it because you want to. If you don't want to lose weight or you don't want to quit gossiping then there is nothing that I can say or God can say or anybody can say that is going to make you stop. Not your husband, not your wife, nobody. You will keep on doing it. Why? Because you want to. "The devil is making me do it." No, he is not. He provides the temptation but you provide the willingness.

You may have been brought up in a home where those things that I mentioned, smoking, drinking, overeating and other things, were a way of life. Everyone in your family was that way and you probably will be also unless you get some different information. Let's bring it over into a spiritual sense. Most of us belonged to some type of church before we were born again. Very few of us were brought up in Christian homes where we were taught the value of the new birth as a child. Very few of us fit into that category. Most of us were members of some type of religious system and thought that by being a member of that religious system our eternal salvation was taken care of. Then one day we discovered that was not the way it was and we had to make a decision based upon our new information. Amen?

God's Word in many areas of your life will be new

166

information and you must take this new information and put it into your life. How do you put it into your life? The way you cause your mind to be renewed is by meditating in God's Word. That is the only way that you can renew your mind. The renewed mind does not happen through prayer, or fasting, or by seeing miracles. It comes by meditating in God's Word. I can renew my mind but I cannot renew your mind. When you hear someone preach, they give you information. But you must take God's promises and meditate in them in order to learn God's ways of doing things. That will cause you to become spiritually minded or to think spiritually or to think like God thinks. *"Charles, that is impossible."* No, it is not. You have His Word. And His Word is His will. God and His Word are inseparable. In the beginning was the Word, the Word was with God and the Word was God. (John 1:1) As you receive God's new information you must meditate upon it.

Let's take prosperity for example. Philippians 4:19, *"My God shall supply all your needs according to His riches in glory by Christ Jesus."* You hear that verse of scripture and it speaks to your heart. "I'm glad to know that. I'm glad that I came to church tonight. I have learned that God wants to help, God wants to meet my needs, He wants to bless me financially, He wants to make sure that all of my bills are paid and there is enough left for me to bless other people." Just hearing that is not enough. For some of us it takes a while to renew our mind. For others it does not. I have seen that in certain areas, some people grasp things faster than other people do but the person that may have a hard time grasping prosperity will grasp some other truth very quickly. That happened to me. I grasped healing very quickly. It made sense to me. I had no trouble believing that God wanted me well. That was the easiest thing in the world for me to believe. God is love. My earthly daddy, when I lived at home, and became sick did everything within his power to heal me, to get me well. It stood to reason to me that if my earthly daddy loved me and he was willing to do anything within his power to get me well, then my heavenly Father, who the Bible says is love, would do anything within His power to make me well. I had no trouble believing that. My mind reasoned in that way, but I had a time with prosperity. I wanted to believe it. I tried to believe it but my mind really fought with me. My mind could not reason that anyone would ever walk up to me and give me money. I could see them doing that to Brother Copeland or Jerry Savelle or Bob Tilton but not for me. You may have had the same problem. You thought, "I can see it happen to Charles and Rochelle but for me — nobody even knows that I'm alive." That is the way I used to think. Then I realized that my mind was fighting me and I had to renew it. I had to give it new information through meditating in God's Word.

This is how you meditate the Word of God. The word meditate has two basic definitions. In the Old Testament the Hebrew definition for the word meditate means to mutter. Literally defined mutter means "to speak to yourself in a low tone of voice." In the New Testament the word meditate means to revolve in the mind. To revolve, not to resolve, to revolve. Like a revolving door. To revolve in the mind.

Philippians 4:19, *"My God shall supply all your needs. . . ."* Here is the process to renew your mind to

168

God's will to bless you financially. You take the scripture *"My God shall supply all your needs. . . "* and on purpose you begin to think about it. You take that thought and you put it in your mind. You can think about anything you want to think about. Your mind is your mind and you can think about what you want to think about. Your thoughts are your thoughts and you can think about anything you want to think about. Your mind is not Satan's territory and it is not God's territory. It is your mind and you can think about what you want. Satan will try to put information into your mind and cause you to think about it and reason upon it. But you choose what type of thoughts you are going to take. They are your thoughts, you choose them, so choose to think God's Word. *"My God shall supply all my needs. . . "* You begin to revolve it in your mind. Joshua 1:8 — God said meditate in the Word day and night. The word meditate literally means mutter, speak to yourself in a low tone of voice. People take these things as laws instead of principles. Meditating is not a law it is a principle.

God was fully aware that when He told Joshua to meditate in the Word day and night that there would be times when Joshua would need to run the nation of Israel and talk to people about other things besides the Word of God. Just as you have times during your day when you cannot be speaking God's Word to yourself or others. You will need to talk to them about different things relating to whatever you do. But in the spare time that you have meditate in the Word. I know people that write verses of scripture on index cards and put them on their mirror so that in the morning they can look at them and they speak them to themselves while they are getting dressed. Instead of turning on the television, meditate in the Word of God. Redeem the time. The word redeem means "make the most of" the time. You may have 30 minutes or an hour. Some ladies take an hour sitting in front of the mirror getting ready. That is an hour you can use to meditate in God's Word, to speak God's Word to yourself. Listen to yourself while you are saying it, and think about it. *"My God shall supply. . . "* Cause the verse to go across your mind as you say it. Romans 10:17 says faith comes by hearing and hearing by the Word of God. As you hear yourself say it faith comes alive in your heart. So actually you are charging yourself up on the inside while you are renewing your mind.

You are actually accomplishing two things at once. You are meditating in the Word and energizing your own human spirit. How do you energize your own human spirit? Be meditating in the Word of God. Speaking the Word to yourself. You build the reality of God's Word into your heart as you speak God's Word to yourself. "How long do I have to do that Charles?" For the rest of your life. "You mean once I get my mind renewed to prosperity I must keep on renewing it." No, you do not keep on renewing your mind, you keep it at that place just because you get your mind renewed to the Word of God in a certain area does not mean Satan's attempt to put contrary information into your mind will stop. There will still be thoughts of lack and need coming at you. You may turn on the news and they will say the country is going under, and everyone is going to lose their house. When your mind is renewed it will fight those thoughts on its own. It will reject those thoughts and when you couple that with the confession of your heart out of your mouth and the promise of God — when David said I was young and I now am old and I've never seen the righteous forsaken or their seed out begging for bread.

Do you see the difference? When your mind is renewed instead of saying, "Oh my God, we are all going broke" — instead of thinking carnally and according to the world's ways of doing things, instead of thinking like the world thinks, you start thinking like God thinks and when you start thinking like God thinks you are going to be in control of your life. Meditate in the Word while you are driving your car. Turn off the silly country western music or rock music. Why are you listening to that garbage anyway? You need to guard your heart. Solomon was not kidding when he wrote in Proverbs 4:23 for us to guard your hearts with all diligence. "I don't understand it Charles, I can't seem to get ahead." What are you doing with your life? Are you putting the Word of God into your life? Do you listen to teaching tapes in your car? Do you listen to good Christian music in your car? Or do you listen to that garbage about drugs and idol worship and things like that? "Oh, they don't sing about that." Bless your heart, you are living in a fairy tale world. And a lot of our children are listening to that garbage. I mean garbage — pure filth, sexual filth and they listen to it over and over. And then people come to church and say "I don't know why my children do the things they do." Because it is in them. It has been programmed into them for years. You need to get them some new information. New information — not just that old garbage.

I want to give you four steps for energizing your apirit. Number one — meditating in the Word of God.

Number two — be a doer of the Word, not just a talker — a doer. Number three — give the Word first place in your life. It will do you a world of good, if you are not already doing it, to start getting up 30 minutes earlier in the morning and pray in the spirit and meditate in God's Word. It will change your life if you will do it. Do not tell me that your body is going to die because it got 11 ½ hours sleep instead of 12. It will survive, I can assure you it will not die. The first couple of days it will tell you that it is going to die, but you can train it. Your body does what your mind tells it to do.

Remember, if you are not making things happen in your life then you are letting things happen, and a good way to make things happen in your life is by praying in the spirit and by confessing God's Word and meditating in the Word of God. I get up quite often in the mornings and pray in the spirit and meditate in the Word of God and do the best that I can to build God's Word down into my heart and release the power of God that is in me. I will be honest with you, a lot of times when I'm walking around in my den I do not feel anything. At times it seems like God is on vacation. He does not say anything. He does not reveal anything to me. He does not even talk to me. That used to bother me. I used to say, "What good is this? Here I am walking around and I don't even think God is listening to me." That is the unrenewed mind moved by feelings. The mind wants feelings. You must go beyond feelings and realize that when you are praying in the spirit and doing the things of God you are making things happen whether you think they are happening or not. Whether you feel like they are happening or not. You are making things happen. It would change your whole life if you started doing that.

Number four — train yourself to instantly obey the voice of your own spirit. Here is everything in summary. This is how it works. First comes the information and then comes meditation and then comes application. Information, meditation, application. Don't try to apply it until you have meditated on it. How does the information come? By reading, observation, studying and listening. Then comes meditation and after you have meditated on it God will reveal to you how to apply it. Information, meditation, application.

Chapter XII

SYMPTOMS OF A MIND
UNDER ATTACK

The mind is a battle ground. That is where the devil originates his attack on the Christian. There is a closeness between the mind of the believer and Satan because it was in the mind that the devil had his original operations before you ever became a child of God. It was in your mind that he first would affect you. II Corinthians 4 says that the devil has blinded the minds of them that believe not. Most of us, for many years, before we made Jesus our Lord became filled with the Holy Spirit and started acting on God's Word and started putting His Word into our hearts, listened to the voice of the devil in our minds and even after we were saved there still exists a special type of a closeness that you need to watch out for. You need to know that it is there and you need to move against it and regain the ground that you have unwillingly and unconsciously given over to Satan through your ignorance of his operations and what and how God deals with you and how Satan operates in the mind of a man. By our being ignorant of these thing, we have unwillingly given ground to him in our minds. Many people today have demonic strongholds in their minds that have been built there through a long succession of suggestions and thoughts and impressions implanted on their minds and through their believing that all supernatural revelation that comes to their mind must be from God. They have opened themselves up and allowed the devil to get a grip on their consciousness. It happens to people every day. The whole plan behind him attacking your mind is to get control of it, thereby gaining control of your will and controlling your life. He wants your mind. He wants to get it and he wants to control it. You are going to have to fight him for it. Just because you are a Christian does not mean that he is going to leave you alone.

Many Christians are unable to distinguish between the activity of evil spirits and the activity of the Holy Spirit and because of that inability to distinguish between them they have unconsciously opened themselves up to the activity of evil spirits. They have actually given them ground.

I want to give you some of the symptoms of a mind that is under attack. One of the major symptoms is flashing thoughts. These thoughts flash into your consciousness and many times they come to you as a special revelation, to give you special information and special understanding that no one else has. You are the only one. "This is a special revelation from God to you. No one else knows it and God is going to use you to shake the entire world, for you are God's chosen vessel.'' I have become very leary of these brothers that come up with special revelation that no one else has. I am particulary leary of them when their mind is made up that they are right and will not receive any reasoning or any counsel because they are convinced that they are right and you are wrong. If you do not see it like they see it then you are wrong, because they are always right. If you start thinking like that you are in trouble. If you reach a point in your life that you cannot receive counsel then you have put yourself in a position to be deceived. That happens when people start listening to voices and allowing their thoughts to run on the thoughts of the devil that are used to puff them up. Those things disarm you, they strip away your weapons, they get you to where you are listening to them and concentrating on them so much that you can not hear the spirit of God and what He is saying. The devil will try to lead you astray. He will try to lead you into a false way.

What did Jesus say the thief comes to do? To steal, kill and to destroy. (John 10:10) Many times people's minds are like perpetual thought machines — it just runs and runs. You may say, ''How do I know when those thoughts are being inspried by a demonic force and not by myself?'' When you purpose within yourself not to think about them and you cannot stop them. You are to be in control of your every ability — spirit, soul and body. If you purpose not to think about a certain thing and the thoughts remain what is it? It is an evil spirit. We are not going demon hunting because if we do we will find one. We are looking at this because we want to understand what these operations are. We need to understand that these perpetual thoughts, when we purpose within ourselves not to think about them anymore, are of the devil.

Have you ever laid down in bed at night and your mind would not allow you to go to sleep? You laid awake all night long and your mind is just running and running and you tell it to be quiet. But it just keeps right on going. That is a sign of demonic activity in your mind. It is not something to be ashamed of, but it is a sign of demonic activity and it can be and should be removed from your consciousness. You lay in bed at night and those thoughts keep running and running, and before you know it you need to get up and you haven't slept and you are tired and irritable and mad at yourself and at God.

"But it just seems to me, that God should be able to do something about this." You need to watch out for self-pity. Self-pity is the biggest gate opener to the devil in the body of Christ. "I don't understand it Lord, I'm out here preaching the Gospel, traveling all over the country, ministering to people, going here and going there. It seems to me the least you could do is heal my body.

"Charles, have you ever had thoughts like that." Yes. When you start feeling sorry for yourself the devil will keep piling it on. That is a demonic force working on you trying to drag you down and pull you under. You do not have to be in the ministry for that to come at you. You can be working on the job or working at home or whatever you want to do and that stuff can come at you. "I don t understand why I don't get the respect or love that I desire!" You can roll around in self-pity all you want, but it will not change anything. Not one thing will change. The things that have been causing the problems will stay until you finally get so fed up with it that you will do one of two things. You quit entirely and give up or you will pick yourself up and get mad at the devil. Hopefully you will do the last one.

Satan will come at you — he comes in many times like light to try to get you to believe, or to understand or discover special matters. We need to watch out for these things. I Timothy 4 talks about things that will occur in these last days. Verse 1, *"Now the Spirit speaketh expressly, that in the latter times some shall depart from the faith. . . "* Did you see that? It said some will depart from the faith. He is not talking about men that are not Christians. He is talking about men that are in the faith. In the faith and they will depart from it. Why? . . . *"giving heed to seducing spirits, and doctrines of devils."* Where do those spirits seduce you? In your mind. Where does the doctrine of the devil come to? Your mind. Do not get the idea that he will come to you saying, "Look this is from the devil." He will wrap it up in a pretty package and put a special bow on it. He will work at you, coming from different directions and get your pride lifted up. He will say, "This is the thing that God would have you to know in order that you might win the world. You are the one that God is going to use to bring the body of Christ together." You are not. You are not going to do it. There have been men down through the years that have tried their best to bring the body of Christ together. The only one that is able to do it is the Spirit of God, and the only way that he will be able to do that is when the people of God start putting God's Word into their hearts and lay down their pride, and self-pity, and selfishness and start acting on God's Word. Then we will come together.

179

You must watch out because the devil is going to use the minds of men in order to propagate his gospel, his doctrines of devils. Another thing that the devil will use is dreams and visions. A dream or a vision can come from one of two ways — either naturally or supernaturally. It can come from yourself. Yes, you can dream things of yourself. David said, *"I purpose that my night meditations will be of the Lord."* There are dreams that can originate within yourself. There are dreams that can come from God. There are dreams that come from the devil. "How do I know the difference between them." A dream or a vision that comes from God will create peace. It will create steadyness. It will be full of reasoning and consciousness. A dream or a vision that comes from the devil is bazaar, rash, fantastic, foolish and it will cause the person to be arrogant, dazed, confused and irrational. It will be so incredible that it is beyond anything you could ever think of. A lot of us have had dreams like that — we call them nightmares. They are bad, they hurt you, and they harm you.

Another sign of demonic influence in the mind is forgetfulness. Many times people's memories fail them at critical times. They may be talking on the phone about something very important and their mind goes blank. That has happened to me while I was preaching. God would show me a point that He wanted me to start working on and I would get right to it and forget where I was going. What do you do then? You start saying on the inside of you, *"The Lord is my shepherd I do not want."* It has happened to me before and it did not come back. I had to go home that night and ask the spirit of God to remind me and then I would write it down in my notes

180

so I could preach it in the next service.

Another sign of demonic influence in the mind is lack of concentration. Many times people will be reading or they will be sitting in a service and be concentrating on something and suddenly their mind will turn blank and wander off for 15 or 20 minutes. I have seen it happen on a lot of people's faces. I know when it is happening because people get a dazed look on their face — and I loose eye contact with them. They may be look at me but it is like they are looking at a picture. Have you ever been talking to someone and suddenly you realized they were not hearing one word you said? Have you ever been reading a book and close it and not have the slightest idea what you read? That happens a lot of times when people read the Word. Many people wrinkle up their foreheads, and squint their eyes trying to concentrate. I have seen people that when they start losing their concentration they would shake their heads and try to shake those thoughts out of their mind. You can't shake those thoughts out of your mind. All that does is make you dizzy. That is not the way God designed the human mind to operate, and anything that is not in accordance with the way God designed it to operate is not right. We want the mind to be what God designed it to be.

Your mind can function on a higher level in a better way. All of us should be experiencing a greater mental capacity than we have ever experienced in our lives. You should be able to remember things that you never could remember. You can discipline your mind so that it will not forget. You can train it, it has that capacity. Medical science says that the average human being uses 10% of his mental capacity. That means the other 90% is laying dormant. Can you imagine how far the human race would be today if we were using 20% instead of 10%? How about 50%? Think of all the marvelous things that we have created and done using 10% of our mental ability. Do you see how far below the level we have lived compared to what God created us for?

Another sign of demonic influence in a person's mind is when they are double-minded. How many times have you seen people that say they are going to do something and then go and do the exact opposite? You think, "Bless their hearts." They do not need their hearts blessed, they need their heads blessed. That is where the problem is. A demon will tell you one thing and get you to move in it and then tell you to do something else, and if you don't do the second then they start condemning you because you are not acting on God's Word. You are not following the leading of the spirit. They will try to get you going back and forth, back and forth like a ping-pong ball.

Another sign of demonic activity in the mind is talkativeness. A mind that can not listen but demands for others to listen to it has problems. Have you ever been talking to somebody and the whole time you are talking you know that they were not listening to one thing you were saying? All they were doing was thinking up things to argue back at you with. They were looking at you and shaking their head but just as soon as you give them a chance, and many times they don't even wait for a chance, they start right in and interrupt what you were saying.

Another sign is obstinancy. Becoming stubborn and refusing to listen to anyone once the decision is made. "I do not need to listen to others because nobody knows as much about this as I do." No, they do not.

In summary there is one principle that underlies everyone of these things. You can lose control of a part of your mind. Once we discover that we are having problems in these areas it is not something to be ashamed of, it is something to correct. You can get free from it. There is a way out. Colossians 1:13 says that we have been delivered from the authority of darkness and translated into the kingdom of God's dear Son in whom we have redemption through His blood even the remission of our sins. Praise God, deliverance is available. I do not care how bad it may be, or how bad some of those symptoms are or how tormented you may be by demonic spirits. There is deliverance. Jesus has provided a way for you to get out. I do not care how big those strongholds are or how great they are or if they have been there for 25, 30, 45, or 50 years. They can be torn down. They can be erased. You can recover the ground that you have lost. You can bring you mind to the place where God designed it to be. It is your right as a human being to be in control of your mind.

The first step is to recognize that your mind is under attack and then you can start doing something about it. But there are a lot of people that are afraid to talk about these things. They are afraid to talk about any type of demonic influence in their life. Do you know why? Because it scares them. It is frightening to them. Many times when you start talking to people about the operation of demonic spirits and the influence that they can have upon people, people will say, "No. I do not believe in demonic spirits. I'm a Christian. They cannot bother me." Those are all cop-outs. I am not saying to worry about them, I am saying to take care of them.

In order to be free from these things there are certain things that you need to do. First of all you need to make a decision that you are going to be free, that you are going to regain that lost ground, that you are going to get control of your mind and you are going to be the one that is in control of it, not the devil. When you make the decision to be free, get ready for some lies to start coming at you. There is nothing quite like a thief when he has been caught. You walk into a room and catch someone with his hand in your money box and get ready for some excuses. They will come at you just as fast as you are willing to listen to them until you say, "Shut up, you are through. I caught you."

As you have been reading this chapter you may have been thinking, "I have been having problems like that. I have had problems in that area. Those things have happened to me before. That is the devil that has been doing that to me and I am going to do something about it." When you turn the light on him, he will not want to leave. You give him expression in the earth. He will not want to leave so he will begin to lie to you. Here are some of the lies that the devil will say to you. He will tell you that those sudden beautiful thoughts are from God. Those flashing revelations that come to you are fruits of your spirituality. "Really, I'm that spiritual? I knew I was all along, and now the fruits of it are coming." Hold it. God is not going to tell you that. God is not going to tell you things like that because it will get your mind puffed up. Another thing that the devil will tell you is that your bad memory is due to ill health. And if that does not get you then he will tell you that you inherited it and there is nothing that can be done about it, so you might as well learn to live with it. That is what he wants you to do — live with it.

Another thing he will say is that the reason you have all these mental problems is because you are overworked. You are over tired. He is trying to blame you. "It is your fault, not my fault," not the devil's fault, it is your fault. If he gets it back on you then you will quit looking at him and he can go back into hiding and cover up his trail and he continues to operate there. Another thing that he will tell you is that it is someone elses' fault. It is their fault, not his fault. The last one and this is the ultimate one, this is one that he will use when everything else fails. "There is no salvation for you because you have fallen from grace. You have gone so far that you have fallen from God's grace and there is no salvation for you." When he cannot fool you with the other things he will try to scare you back into your corner and get you to accept it. What do you do when those thoughts come? You check them out according to the Word of God.

The Word of God is the light and you need to keep the light on in order to dispel the darkness. By keeping God's light on it will bring it to the front and you will see what it is and be able to move against it with the weapons that God has provided. If you are going to receive deliverance from these things you need to realize that your weapons are going to need to be spiritual and not carnal. Making vows and resolutions will not change them. You will need to come at these things with the weapons of your warfare which 11 Corinthians 10:4 and 5 says are not carnal but mighty through God for the pulling down of strongholds. Spiritual weapons. We are not going at this in a physical way. You can make all the resolutions and all the vows and all the good plans that you want, but until you move against these things with the power of the spirit and use the Word of God and the sword of the spirit and attack these things with God's Word you will not receive freedom from them in any form. They will deceive you into thinking that you are free. They will back off and be quiet for awhile and then come back. You need to realize and recognize that you have been attacked and that you are not in the normal state for which you were created and you need to purpose within yourself to become into that state of normalcy that God has designed the human mind to be in.

There are three ways that a mind gets occupied and three ways that it gets delivered. One way that a mind becomes occupied is when it is unrenewed. The other way is that it accepts the lies of evil spirits. The third way is through passivity. A passive mind is a mind that does not originate thought on its own but merely waits like a dry sponge for things to come into it from on the outside. It takes all supernatural thoughts as being from God. I told you in earlier chapters that God does not reveal His will to your mind. He reveals it to your spirit and your spirit communicates it to your mind, your mind relays it to your will, your will tells your body. God is a spirit. He uses His spirit Word to reveal Himself in your spirit. "But how can I ever learn to discern between what is coming into my mind and what is coming into my spirit?" The only way you will be able to discern between the operation of the soul and the operation of the spirit is by God's Word dwelling in you richly, because it is the only thing that can divide them apart. Your spirit and soul are closely tied together. They are so much alike and operate so much together that they look like they are one in the same. For that reason many people consider them the same. Most people use the words interchangeably. But they are not supposed to be used interchangeably. They are different. They have different functions. They are created different. They operate in different realms, but they operate together. The soul and the spirit are to operate together and the only thing that can divide them asunder is God's Word dwelling in you richly.

Hebrews 4:12 — The Word of God is sharp and powerful, sharper than any two-edged word and will divide asunder the soul and the spirit and the joints and the marrow. God's Word will do it. Medical science can not do it. Psychology can not do it. They have recognized that there is somebody else in there. They have recognized there is somebody else in that being that they are talking to. What do they call him — the subconscious. What is he? The spirit. They say, "These things come out of the subconscious and we do not know how that operate, or why it operates, but it affects you." That is why you will receive little permanent help from the world. You will receive help — no question about that. But I tell you right now that unless that person you are talking to is operating in God's Word he will not be able to get to the root. He may teach you how to control the problem, but it will manifest someplace else.

An example of this is people that quit smoking. They discipline themselves not to give in to smoking anymore and the next thing you know they gain 75 pounds. What about that? That will happen until you get to the root. Until you attack the root of a weed you will have weeds.

You can cut them off all summer long but until somebody goes out and digs up the root they will be there. And the bad thing about it is they spread. Until you get to the root you will not get control of the weed.

The three ways that a mind is regained or delivered is by renewing of the mind, the denying of the lies, and the over-turning of the passivity. That can be hard for some Christians because they have worked many hours on getting their minds into a passive state because they believe that is the way it must be before God can talk to them.

Let's talk about renewing the mind. Romans 12:1, *"I beseech you therefore, brethren, by the mercies of God, that ye present your bodies a living sacrifice, holy, acceptable unto God, which is your reasonable service. And be not conformed to this world: but be ye transformed by the renewing of your mind, that ye may prove what is that good, and acceptable, and perfect, will of God."* What did he say to do with your mind? He said to renew it. What will happen when you get your mind renewed? You will be transformed from the world. You will not be of the world anymore. We do not want to be conformed to the world. You do not want to think like the world thinks. You want to think like God thinks. How do you get your mind renewed to God's Word? Some people would have you to believe that the way to do that is to have someone lay hands on you and ask God to heal your memory. That does not do any good. He said for us to renew our mind.

Ephesians 4:17, *"This I say therefore, and testify in the Lord, that ye henceforth walk not as other Gentiles walk, in the vanity of their mind, Having the under-*

standing darkened, being alienated from the life of God through the ignorance that is in them, because of the blindness of their heart." He said he does not want us to walk as the other Gentiles walk which proves to us that it is possible to do it.

In verse 23 he says for you to be renewed in the spirit of your mind and put off the old man and put on the new man which is after God and is created in righteousness and true holiness. What did he say to do? He said to be renewed in the spirit of your mind and put off concerning the former conversation the old man. Put off the old man thoughts, quit thinking like the old man thinks. Make your mind think a new way, make your mind think according to God's Word, make your mind reason according to God's Word. "You can not reason with God's Word." Sure you can. In the book of Isaiah God said *"Come let us reason together, saith the Lord."* God will reason with you but He does not reason according to the world's standards. God's Word makes sense. When it does not make sense to you is when you get little portions of it and try to make your mind believe it.

You need to be renewed in your mind. How are you going to do it? The first thing you do it put off the old man. Put off the old way of thinking. Quit thinking about the things that you used to think about before you got saved. Think new. Renew your mind, put new thoughts in it. What you are doing is regaining the territory that you have lost. Take it back and say, "No, this is mine," and bring it back. Then look and if you see another stronghold, attack that one and pull that one down and get that land back.

The renewing of the mind is vitally important. Why

does the mind need to be renewed? Romans 8:6, *For to be carnally minded is death . . . "* That literally says, *"For the minding of the flesh is death but the minding of the spirit is life and peace because the minding of the flesh is enmity against God for it is not subject to the law of God, neither indeed can be."* Your mind, before it becomes renewed to God's Word, is in enmity against God. All it has ever listened to is the flesh or the things of this world. The new birth does not affect the mind — affects the spirit. The indwelling of the Holy Spirit does not take place in the mind, it takes place in the spirit. You are then to take God's Word and use it to renew your mind. You do that by putting the Word before your eyes, and inclicing your ears unto it, and by speaking it out of your mouth and allowing the Word to dwell richly in you.

Your mind will like operating on God's Word when you give it a chance. We need to get our minds renewed because the carnal mind, the mind that came with us after the new birth, is in enmity with God. It is not in line with God's Word. It is not subject to the law of God and it can not be subject to the law of God. "What is the solution then?" You say, "Well what do we do to help us here?" Romans 6:11, *"Likewise reckon ye also yourselves to be dead indeed unto sin, but alive unto God through Jesus Christ our Lord."* What did he say to do? He said to reckon yourself — reckoning takes place where? In the mind. Begin reckoning yourself to be dead to those old thoughts, see yourself dead to those old thoughts. See yourself separated from them — you are going to have to do that. Before you are going to be free of demonic influence in your mind you need to first make the decision that you are separate from them, they are not your thoughts. As long as you align yourself with those thoughts they will stay there. Satan will try to get you to think that it was you that was Thinking that way and if he can get you to thinking that it was you then the thoughts will remain because you have activated your will into believing that they are yours and you will not resist them. You must look at them and draw a line and say, "That is of God and that is of the devil. I am over here with God and I am resisting that which is of the devil." Do you understand that. You must separate yourself from it. You have to free yourself from it. You must separate yourself. When you do that then you begin operating against them, but as long as you consider the possibility that they are actually of you and not of the devil then they will remain there.

"...reckon ye also yourselves to be dead indeed unto sin..." Dead to sin. "Praise God, that is not of me, it is of the devil. Those are not my thoughts, those are Satan's thoughts. I died the death of the cross, those things are not of me — they are of Satan!" Do you see what I'm saying? Verse 12, *"Let not sin therefore reign in your mortal body, that ye should obey it in the lusts thereof."* You need to reckon yourself dead to sin and turn on it and say, "You are not going to reign on me any more. You are not going to operate here. You are through in my life."

11 Corinthians 10:3, *"For though we walk in the flesh, we do not war after the flesh: (For the weapons of our warfare are not carnal, but mighty through God to the pulling down of strong holds.), Casting down imaginations, and every thigh thing that exalteth itself*

191

against the knowledge of God, and bringing into captivity every thought to the obedience of Christ; And having in a readiness to revenge all disobedience, when your obedience is fulfilled." Praise God! That is how you attack. You attack every thought that comes into your consciousness and you make it line up with the Word of God. You make it become obedient to Jesus Christ and if it does not become obedient to Him and to what the Word says then it is of the devil and you are to cast it out of you using the mighty name of Jesus and the faith of God that He has placed within your spirit to use against the onslaught of the wicked one. Use these weapons that God has given to you and placed at your disposal. Notice, He said that you are to cast them down. Don't ask God to tear them down for you. He is not going to do it. You do it. He has given you the weapons to do it. The thoughts are coming into your head, so you deal with them. God has given you the weapons. You are not limited to carnal weapons.

I Corinthians 10:13, *"There hath no temptation taken you but such as is common to man: but God is faithful, who will not suffer you to be tempted above that ye are able; but will with the temptation also make a way to escape, that ye may be able to bear it."* The devil only has temptations that are common to man. But God has provided a way out for you and what does he say our weapons are in II Corinthians 10? He said the weapons of our warfare are not carnal, not common to man but are from God. God has provided a way out for you from every temptation that the devil brings against you. There is nothing that Satan can bring against you that God has not provided a way and a means and a weapon to use to get out of it. I can prove it to you in Ephesians 6. Paul said the shield of faith is able to quench all the fiery darts of the wicked. Not some, but all! I John 5:4 says this is the victory that becomes the world, even our faith. I Corinthians 13:8 says love never fails. You have two things that will win everytime — faith and love. They will win everytime, not counting righteousness, or assurance, or peace, or joy, or gentleness, or long suffering, or meekness, or goodness, or temperance. He said against all those things there is no law or there is nothing that can overcome those nine forces. Do you see it? God has provided a means of escape. How do you do it? You examine every thought that comes into your mind and not allow any thought to go unattended. If it shows up, deal with it. I don't care how silly it looks, deal with it. You are the one that is going to be the deciding factor in how much control you gain in your mind and what is going on in it. You are the one that is going to decide how pure, clear and clean your mind is going to be. You are the one that is going to decide how renewed your mind is going to become. You are the one that is going to decide how much ability you are going to draw out of your mind. You are the one that is going to decide all those things and you are going to have to start doing them today. It's all there. It's all available to you — God has presented it all to you. Now what are you going to do with it? Are you going to go at it 10%, 20%, 80% or are you going to go all the way and deal with everything that comes and demand that your mind become renewed to the Word of God, completely and totally in every segment of your life? It can be done and it is worth it.

Chapter XIII

OVERCOMING STRONGHOLDS IN YOUR MIND

We have been studying the various affects the mind has. The mind is a component of the soul. The soul stands between the spirit man and the body or the flesh and is used to bring them together. We have seen the God reveals Himself to the spirit of a man and the spirit thereby enlightens what it has received or what has been revealed to the mind. The mind is to judge, discern, look at, reason, pick at, pick apart, and gauge all the thoughts that come into it. It is not supposed to receive things passively because not every thought that comes supernaturally is from God. God does do things supernaturally, no question that is His way. He is a supernatural being. But there is another supernatural being loose in this planet by the name of the devil, Satan, the old serpent, the deceiver as the Book of Revelations calls him. He is here to try to deceive you and lead you astray. He does that by attacking your mind. The mind is the battle ground — the battle field — that is where he will launch his attack. That is where he brings his thoughts. His temptations will always come to you in the form of a thoughts.

We have seen that we all have been given the God-given ability to rule and control our minds. They are not to run on us, they are not to be uncontrolled, they are not to be stagnet, they are not to be totally quiet, or open to any thought that comes and we are not to think that every thought is of God unless it has "devil" written all over it in black and white. A lot of people are open to the things of Satan because he has deceived them into thinking that they are the things of God when they are not. The devil will try to lead you astray and try to get you to where you are listening to voices. There are people that listen to voices all the time. They are open to them constantly, listening for a voice. There are other beings in the earth that are speaking and they will speak to you. They will say things that sound good. They may even quote scripture to try to lead you astray. "I can't believe that." Then remember what he did in Luke 4 with Jesus. Satan quoted the 91st Psalm, but he took it out of context and tried to get Jesus to use it incorrectly.

The devil is no fool. At the same time he is not real bright. He has no new tricks, everything is the same. If has has done something to one man he will try to do it to another. If I have heard it, you are going to hear it. He may put a different color bow on it, but it is the same package. But I Corinthians 10 says that the devil can use no temptation against us but that which is common to man. And II Corinthians 10 says that the weapons of our warfare are not common to man but mighty through God for the pulling down of strongholds. The devil is limited and we are not. He can only use things that are common to this planet but we can tap into the resources of heaven and cause a mighty onslaught against his kingdom and bring forth an abundant harvest from it. The devil is getting weaker all the time. He is not getting any new recruits. He is constantly losing people. His kingdom is constantly losing people because they are coming out of that kingdom, and he can't go anywhere to recruit new ones. His kingdom is getting smaller and God's kingdom is getting bigger.

There is a battle going on in the earth today between God and Satan and many people have the impression that in this battle God and Satan are almost equal in ability and in power. They think Satan is almost an equal being with God. They think God is going to need to stay on His toes to win because the devil has a lot of power and a lot of ability and is just like God Himself. That is a lie right out of the pit of hell. The devil is not even near God's class. He was created by God, an inferior being. When he was in his highest state, he was inferior to God. When he fell he went below that level. He is a fallen angel. Satan was made as a servant of God. He was not made to fellowship with God. He was not made to live in harmony with God. He was made to be God's servant. He was deceived by his own beauty. He said, "I should be God." That did it. He was gone. The Bible says that before his fall he was called Lucifer and that his very wings shadowed the throne of God. He was the anointed cherub and he shadowed the throne of God. He stood above the throne. He was as close as you could get to the God-head but he was not the God-head. Remember that because he will always try to puff himself up and cause you to think that he has so much power and ability. That is a lie of the devil.

Now as children of God we are so far above him. The power and the ability that is born into us as children of the living God is far superior to the abilities that he has. He is a master deceiver. He has been deceiving people for 7,000 years. He has got a kingdom set up. He has principalities and powers and rulers of the darkness and spiritual wicked spirits in heavenly places, but we've been given the keys to the gates of hell! We have been given the keys to the kingdom of God. We have been given the mighty name of Jesus and at the sound of that name every knee must bow and every tongue must confess that Jesus Christ is Lord to the glory of God, the Father, of beings in heaven, beings in earth, beings under the earth. There is nothing that can stand up to the matchless name of Jesus.

I don't care how long the devil has built up a stronghold in a person's life, you can step in and instantly see him set free with the power of the name of Jesus. There is nothing that compares to that name. In Hebrews it is called the more excellent name. There may be a name that is good, but we have one that is more excellent than that. You may know a name that is powerful, we have one that is more excellent than that. You may know a name that is famous, we have one that is more excellent than that. You may have a name that is associated with conquest, we have one that is more excellent than that. You may have a name that carries authority, but we have one that is more excellent than that. The name of Jesus. It has been given to us as a weapon.

I went into all that to bring you to this point. We have learned that the devil wants to gain control of your mind, thereby gaining control of your will. The way he will gain control of your mind is by getting ground in your mind. He will try to take it from you through seeding your mind with bad information. There is a law in the spirit realm that you must understand and act upon if you are going to recover that territory you have lost, and that law is that the devil can do nothing to you but what you allow to be done. If you are going to regain the territory that you have lost to him in your mind, the first thing you must do is set your will to get it back. When you do that he is on his way out. Regain that ground.

In the previous chapter I told you that there are three things that you need to do to get your mind back in control and to get delivered from demonic influence. First you must get your mind renewed. Romans chapter 12 tells us to renew our minds so that we will not be conformed to this world. II Corinthians chapter 4 calls Satan the god of this world. We do not want to be conformed to the world but we want to be transformed of it, we want to be in the world but not of it. We do not want to be of this world. We must set out as Paul said in Ephesians 4 and be renewed in the spirit or in the attitudes of our minds. We do not want our minds to be a play ground. We want them to be used the way they were designed to be used. We want them to function the way they were designed to function. We do not allow the devil to merely come across our minds anytime he pleases and deposit his seeds and be gone. The mind is fertile ground and the devil knows how to use it, but praise God, the spirit of God designed it. He put it together and He is an expert at what will cause it to function at it's highest level, so we want to be renewed in the spirit of our mind. We want our minds to be free and we desire our minds to be renewed. I not only want my mind free of demonic influence I want it renewed to the ways of God. I want it to think like God thinks.

A lot of the things that I do now and the way that I live now, five years ago my mind could not understand. When I would see something in God's Word and it was revealed to my spirit, my mind would fight it. But through putting God's Word into my mind and be allowing my mind to go to the Word and look at it and take it apart and study it, my mind has come to the point that it no longer argues with my spirit. The way I live does not seem so far out to me anymore. It makes a lot of sense to me now. To pray to God and ask Him to supply my needs makes sense to me. It may not make sense to you, but it does make sense to me. Why? Because my mind has become renewed in that area. That is available to all of us.

The next thing we need to do in order to regain the territory that we have lost, is to deny the lies that have been put into our minds. Jesus said that Satan is a liar and the father of all lies and there is no truth in him. Anything that he tells you is a lie. He will not tell you the truth. He will lie to you. What he says may be close to the truth but it is still a lie. When you decide that you are going to regain the control of your mind, you will need to attack those lies and deny them. There are people today that believe the lie from the pit of hell that it is not God's will to heal the sick, and a lot of people have had to deny that lie. What is the weapon to use against a lie? The truth. The truth will dispel a lie just like light dispels darkness.

Everything that I'm telling you about recovering the territory that has been lost, you are going to get it out of the Word of God or you are not going to get it. The reason that God wants you to get it out of His Word is because then it is lasting, it is eternal, it is established. The Word has been established, it is unchangeable. It is the same all the time. I am glad my Bible does not change from morning to night.

You need to attack the lies, one at a time. Once you begin to recover the territory you have lost, do not relent until you have obtained complete and total victory. II John verse 8 says for us to be careful that we lose not the things that we have gained. Do not be content until you have gained absolute and total victory.

Lies come in three forms. Thoughts, imaginations and arguments. Do not get in a argument with the devil. You will not win. It is not that you will lose but that you cannot win. You cannot argue with him, because he will admit that you are right. Everything that you say to him he will say that is not true. Do not try to argue with him. Jesus did not argue with the devil in Luke chapter 4. He said, "It is written." He let the Word stand alone. He did not try to prove it. He did not try to back it up. He said, "It is written." Do not argue with him. A lot of Christians do that when they go casting out demons.

I want to give you the characteristics of how your mind should be. II Timothy 1:7, *"For God hath not given us the spirit of fear, but of power, and of love, and of a sound mind."* God has given you that which is required for your mind to be sound. You are to have a sound mind. An established mind. A solid mind. One that is sound and whole. What are the characteristics of a sound mind? The

201

first characteristic of a sound mind is one that is open to teaching. There are a lot of people that are close minded. I am not telling you to run around and stick your ears under everything that is being taught. The same Bible that says for you to have a teachable spirit also says for you to take heed what you hear. You need to read all scripture in the light of other scripture. "1 don't know what I'm supposed to do then, so I'll just stay home." What is that people refuse to take responsibility upon themselves? It may require them getting quiet for ten minutes and listening to the spirit of God to see if they should become involved in what is going on or not. But for some people that is too much effort. You need to be open to teaching — your mind needs to be open to teaching. Do not have preconceived ideas. A lot of times I will not tell anyone what I am going to teach on before I teach because if they know sometimes they get preconceived ideas and then they do not hear what I am going to say. You need to have an open mind, and be teachable, and willing to receive.

The next thing you need is a controlled mind. Your mind needs to be controlled. Thought is the seed of action. Thought comes to produce the harvest of action. Thought is the seed of action, so we want to control our thoughts. I Peter 1:13, *"Wherefore gird up the loins of your mind, be sober, and hope to the end for the grace. . . "* He said gird them up — gird up the loins of your mind. The word gird brings out the idea that he is telling you something that is not going to be easy to do. Who is going to do it? God? The Holy Ghost? Jesus? The angels? Who is going to do it? "You. What are you going to do? You are going to gird up the loins of your mind.

When? Today. "But Charles, I'm too tired to do it today." That is the devil telling you that. He is going to try to pass it off as your problem. "You've been working too hard. You don't have control of your mind because you are over worked or you inherited it." You need to gird up the loins of your mind.

II Corinthians 10 again. It is important that you see these things in your Bible. Refresh your memory with them. Verse 3, *"For though walk in the flesh; we do not war after the flesh: (For the weapons of our warfare are not carnal, but mighty through God to the pulling down of strong holds;) Casting down imaginations, and every high thing that exalteth itself against the knowledge of God, and bringing into captivity every thought to the obedience of Christ."* You can not let anything go by unattended. You need to deal with every thought that comes into your mind. Why? Because thought is the seed of action. When? Five years later? No, when it comes. It is a lot easier to dig up an oak tree when it is an acorn than after it has been there a hundred years. You want to deal with it when it is but a seed, because if you let it take root you have problems. We have all seen pictures of when hurricanes hit an area and how houses are leveled and old oak trees are still standing. They have roots deep down in the ground — they are established. They are established to standing up to hurricanes. The same thing is true with thoughts. They come as a seed and if you will deal with them when they are still a seed then you can get rid of them. But if you allow them to get embedded down into your mind then they are harder to get out. The devil knows a few things about farming also. He will start watering those seeds and they will grow up.

Then you will wish that you had taken care of them before. Now it is true you can still overcome them but it requires more work.

Hebrews 12:1, *"Wherefore seeing we also are compassed about with so great a cloud of witnesses, let us lay aside every weight, and the sin which doth so easily beset us and let us run with patience the race that is set before us, Looking unto Jesus the author and finisher of our faith; who for the joy that was set before him endured the cross, despising the shame, and is set down at the right hand of the throne of God. For consider him that endured such contradiction of sinners against himself, lest ye be wearied and faint in your minds."* What is the sin that so easily besets us? Growing weary and fainting in our minds. You see your spirit man will go and go and go in the things of God but until your mind is girded up and you are looking unto Jesus and considering him you will faint in your mind. Unless the mind is considering Jesus it will grow weary and tired and faint. Your mind needs to work, but it also needs to rest. Your mind needs to get quiet — it needs to rest. How do you do that? Isaiah 26:3 says, *"You keep him in perfect peace whose mind is stayed on thee."* Peace in your mind. How do you get it? By putting it on Jesus. Considering Him. Thinking about the Word, dwelling on it, making your mind stay on the Word. Make it think on the Word, make it consider Him — Jesus.

Philippians 4:6, *"Be careful for nothing; but in every thing by prayer and supplication with thanksgiving let your requests be made known unto God. And the peace of God, which passeth all understanding, shall keep your hearts and minds through Christ Jesus."* What did it say it would keep? It said it would keep your heart and your mind. The peace of God. Yes, God's peace passes all understanding. You can be peaceful in the midst of a storm.

The next state your mind needs to be in is to be full of God's Word. Hebrews 8:10, *"For this is the covenant that I will make with the house of Israel after those days, saith the Lord; I will put my laws into their mind, and write them in their hearts. . . "* God desires that your mind be full of His Word. How are you going to get that? It is vitally important that you memorize scripture. Many people have trouble memorizing scripture. I will show you the easiest way to memorize scripture that I have ever discovered. I have people come to me and say, "How do you know all that scripture? How can you quote all of it? I've been trying to memorize scripture five years and I can't even remember John 3:16." I used to sit at my desk and try to memorize scripture. Once I decided that I was going to memorize 10 verses a day. I would memorize all ten of them, close my book and try to quote them and I could not remember the first one. I was so frustrated and I grew weary and tired and fainted in my mind. But then I learned a way to memorize scripture. Start praying it and you will never forget it. Form prayers out of scripture and you will never forget it — because then it has become an excercise of your mind and your spirit together and it gets burned into your consciousness, because then it is a living thing instead of just letters. God wants scripture to be alive to you and the quickest way you will ever memorize scripture is to pray it. It will be with you.

The last thing you want is a clean mind. It would be

nice if we could take them out and scrub them. The best way I know to do that is go to the spirit of God and say, "If there is anything in my mind that is not supposed to be in here I want you to let me know about it because I am going to clean it up." Paul wrote Timothy and said in a great house there are vessels unto honor and vessels unto dishonor. There are vessels of gold and silver and vessels of earth and mud. But if any man shall purge himself he shall be a vessel unto honor, meet or able for the masters use. You may be a little clay pot in the kingdom of God but you can purge yourself and become a vessel of gold. You can do it and the best way to do it is to turn to God and say, "Anything in me that needs to be cleaned up you let me know, and show me how, and I will do it." Before you pray that prayer think about it, because God will take you at your word. He may show you some things you would like to think He doesn't know about. If He shows you something that is wrong then change it, do not feel embarrassed about it. It is vitally important that you receive God's forgiveness because I John 1:9 says you confess your sins, he is faithful and just to cleanse you from all unrighteousness. I want to get God's cleansing action in this with me. How is God going to clean you up? You are cleansed through the washing of the water by the Word.